READ IT WITH A GRAIN OF SALT

THE TRUTH ABOUT CANADIAN FOOD LABELS FROM AN INDUSTRY INSIDER

Allison Jorgens, B.Sc., P.H.Ec.

D1470467

BD Marketers Press Inc.

Library and Archives Canada Cataloguing in Publication

Jorgens, Allison, 1976-
    Read it with a grain of salt : the truth about Canadian
food labels from an industry insider / Allison Jorgens.

Includes bibliographical references and index.
Issued also in electronic format.
ISBN 978-0-9879563-0-9

    1. Processed foods--Labeling--Canada. 2. Processed
foods--Canada--Marketing. 3. Food industry and
trade--Canada. I. Title.

TX551.J67 2012   613.2   C2012-901383-8

Design and layout by Heidy Lawrance, WeMakeBooks.ca
Cover design by Cynthia Cake, WeMakeBooks.ca
Author photograph by David Topping, David Topping Photography
Edited by Andrea Lemieux
Index by Judith Brand

BD Marketers Press Inc.
7030 Woodbine Ave., Suite 500
Markham, Ontario, Canada
L3R 6G2

Printed and bound in Canada

Dedication

To my wonderful husband, Scott, and my two sweet baby boys, Brandon and Ashton. Thank you for your support, motivation, patience, and love during the writing process.

To the food companies I have worked with in a regulatory capacity, thank you for your diligence in ensuring your labels were accurate according to Canadian regulations. Your commitment to providing Canadian consumers with correct and truthful information on your food labels is commendable, and I hope you will continue to place the health of Canadians as a top priority in your marketing strategies.

To consumers, who are confused, frustrated, intimidated, and overwhelmed with Canadian food labels, I hope this book will empower you with the information you need to make more healthful and informed choices when shopping.

Contents

**Part 3: How to Effectively Read Prepackaged Processed Food
    Labels**

Icons Used in This Book

THE FOLLOWING FOUR ICONS HAVE BEEN used throughout the book to highlight key points, and interesting facts and anecdotes, about prepackaged processed food labels:

1. **Did you know?** The ⚹ icon represents the question "Did you know?" Perhaps you will find the answer to one of your questions about prepackaged processed food labels here!

2. **Caution!** The ⬦ icon highlights facts and information that you may wish to take into greater consideration when shopping.

3. **Quick Tip.** The ✓ icon highlights quick tips that may help to make label reading more efficient!

4. **The Inside Scoop.** The 🍁 icon directs you to additional insights and information available in the "Inside Scoop" section of the "Read It with a Grain of Salt" website: www.grainofsalt.ca.

Introduction

IN ALL FACETS OF OUR LIVES, WE LOOK for quick fixes: ways to save time, ways to save money, and there is no exception when it comes to what we eat. Grocery stores are dominated by prepackaged processed foods (typically, foods packaged in cans, bottles, boxes, cartons, pouches, and bags), and consumers embrace the simplicity such foods offer in their hectic lives. Food companies know that consumers look for wholesome, natural foods, and they have become experts at developing and marketing a variety of imposter products trying to imitate the real deal. Unfortunately, in many cases the disadvantages of prepackaged processed foods far outweigh the advantages, and it is often impossible for the average consumer to know at a glance if the food inside a package meets their criteria for healthful eating.

Most average consumers focus on a poorly understood nutrition facts table, and on claims that may or may not be truthful or meaningful, to make their purchasing decisions. The goal of this book is to educate and empower you to read food labels effectively as an "insider" and "with a grain of salt," and thus avoid falling victim to manipulative marketing, as food companies try to exploit many of the "grey areas" within the regulations in order to better market their products.

After working as a food label specialist in Canada for nearly a decade, I have made it my mission to help decode food labels for consumers from an insider's perspective. I have seen everything from diligent companies trying to follow and abide by the written rule, to companies intentionally mislabelling their foods. Not only have I helped food companies to clean up their labels to avoid having their products pulled from shelves, but I have also provided guidance to them on ways to improve their marketing competitiveness while still abiding by government regulations.

It is these insights that I hope will make *Read It with a Grain of Salt* a valuable resource for consumers who wish to empower themselves with the knowledge and awareness needed to make more healthful and informed choices.

I am always fascinated with behind-the-scenes looks into other industries, and I believe you will be fascinated, and perhaps shocked, with the insights and stories I share in this book.

When you are grocery shopping, you don't always have time to read food labels carefully and thoroughly. I used to spend hours looking for innovative new products, comparing food labels, and looking for more healthful products, but now that I have two little boys, my grocery shopping trips have changed. Long gone are the days of browsing the grocery store; now my goal is to get in and out before jars are broken, diapers are filled, and tears are shed. Whatever your time constraints may be, it is my aim to provide you with the knowledge you need so that the precious moments that you do have to invest in reading labels can be used as efficiently as possible.

This book is not about preaching what you should or should not eat, and it is not about giving you health or nutrition advice, but rather, it is about teaching you how to understand the information and misinformation on prepackaged processed food labels so that you are better equipped to make the decisions that are right for you.

Happy food label reading!
Allison Jorgens

Part 1

The Prepackaged Processed Food Industry

CHAPTER 1

The Players

The Government, the Food Companies,

and You, the Consumer

WHEN IT COMES TO FOOD LABELS FOR prepackaged processed foods sold in Canada, there are three major players: the Canadian government, the food companies, and you, the consumer. A fourth though minor player working behind the scenes are food label specialists such as myself, who are employed by the food companies to ensure compliance with government regulations, while also attempting to represent you, the consumer.

In Canada, governing food safety, under which food labels fall, are two main government organizations: Health Canada and the Canadian Food Inspection Agency (CFIA). In general, Health Canada makes the rules and the CFIA enforces them. It is easy to point fingers at the government, to blame them for what I see as an epidemic of poorly labelled Canadian food products consisting of confusing and potentially misleading claims. But at the end of the day, it isn't so much the rules and government's limited resources to enforce them as it is the food companies' continual efforts to bend and push the limits by exploiting the "grey areas" within the rules in order to sell you their products.

I use the term *food companies* to represent the various manufacturers, importers, distributors, and private-label producers of prepackaged processed foods who design, develop, market, and, ultimately, sell you the prepackaged processed foods that you consume day to day. The Canadian grocery industry is a multi-billion dollar industry, and the sale of prepackaged processed foods is very competitive and very profitable for those who are able to succeed. Many of the leaders within the industry spend millions of dollars in marketing, advertising, packaging, and new-product development in order to persuade you, the consumer, to buy their products over those of their competitors.

As a food label specialist and a consumer, I am a true supporter of the government's effort to create rules for food labels that are intended to protect consumers. Even given the grey areas within the regulations, in theory, consumers are further protected by the mantra: **Thou shall not mislead the consumer or display untruthful, fraudulent, or deceptive information.**[1] The CFIA offers a voluntary label review service to food companies for free; however, most food companies do not use this service because of slow turnaround times and a fear that their products may be flagged for a violation.

---

1. Department of Justice Canada. *Food and Drugs Act*, "Part I, Food," Subsection 5(1).

Did you know?

Although the CFIA offers a voluntary label review service for most food labels, it is still mandatory for food companies to submit their labels for meat products (both domestic and imported) and domestic processed fruit and vegetable products to the CFIA for review and approval before they are able to sell their products in Canada. Keep in mind, however, that just because the information on these labels may be reviewed and approved by the CFIA does not necessarily mean it will not still be confusing or potentially misleading.

Although manufacturers of domestic processed fruit and vegetable products, such as canned and frozen fruits and vegetables, must submit labels for review and approval, those who import processed fruit and vegetable products do not; this seems backwards to me. Always remember to check the country-of-origin statement on processed fruit and vegetable products, and if you do not see "Product of Canada," read the label with a grain of salt.

For food companies, the development of a new product (or redevelopment of an existing product) from conception to eventually getting their products onto store shelves can be a long and costly effort. They often start off with a concept, and then work on developing a recipe, sourcing ingredients, and holding sensory tasting panels to evaluate the palatability of the food. At this point, it may be necessary to tweak the recipe and start the process over. Ingredients are manipulated to ensure nutrient values are within desirable ranges, and a marketing strategy is developed. It is at this stage that work begins on the label. The label is just about always the last piece of months, sometimes years, of work, and many food companies rush through label development in anticipation of getting their products into stores. Any delay in the development cycle is seen as a significant cost for the food company, and although it is always better to "do it right the first time," some companies are okay with just getting it done and dealing with any ramifications later.

Food companies know that they are responsible for ensuring their food is safe and correctly labelled, and that it meets all regulatory requirements; however, they also know that the CFIA is generally understaffed and overworked and does not have the time or resources to review every label found on Canadian store shelves. The conundrum of following the written word versus bending the rules comes down to an evaluation of risk. I have been caught in the middle of risk analyses more often than I would like to admit. How much will we sell with a misleading claim, statement, or declaration versus without it? What will the CFIA's corrective action involve? Overstickering? New labels? A full recall? Will we ever get caught?

I don't want you to think that the government has left you out in the cold. Often harmless but potentially misleading claims slip through the cracks because, as I understand it, the CFIA prioritizes their enforcement efforts based on threats to human health. When it comes to food labels, human health can be threatened when allergens are mislabelled, ingredients that are not permitted in foods in Canada are added to foods, additives with maximum allowable amounts surpass upper limits, nutrients that may be detrimental to human health are inaccurately declared on the nutrition facts table, and nutrient or health claims are incorrect, implying a food is more healthful for you than it actually is.

The CFIA enforcement efforts can range from sending a nonconformance letter to a food company asking them to provide their steps for corrective action, to a full recall of a product from grocery shelves and the mandatory disposal of the food. When there is any interruption in the sales cycle of a food product, companies lose money. Depending on the degree of the nonconformance, they could lose all of their exist-

 Did you know?

Did you know that you can contact the CFIA if you have a complaint? On average, the CFIA receives 2,000 reports from consumers concerning food safety issues each year.* The CFIA uses the information you provide to determine if the product poses a food-safety risk and identifies if any follow-up action is necessary. If the CFIA believes there is a food-safety risk, they conduct an investigation that determines the method of enforcement they will use with the company. It is my understanding that they will not only potentially look into the issue you have identified, but they will also contact you when the investigation is complete to let you know the outcome.

* Canadian Food Inspection Agency. "Statistics: Consumer Food Safety Complaints," June 22, 2011, www.inspection.gc.ca/english/corpaffr/relations/res/statconse.shtml.

ing product as well as their retailers' and consumers' trust in their brand; this degree of loss would be devastating to a food company and could potentially even put them out of business. For this reason, food companies are generally diligent when it comes to claims that may be detrimental to public health.

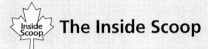

The Inside Scoop

Visit the "Inside Scoop" page at www.grainofsalt.ca and type in the password KNOWLEDGE to gain access. Refer to the "Speak Up!" section for instructions on how to contact the CFIA.

Between the three major players—the government, the food companies, and you, the consumer, ultimately, it is you, the consumer, who has the choice of which products you buy. The government has set the rules, the food companies try to play within them, and presuming that food safety is a top priority for CFIA enforcement, what is left are the "grey areas" within the regulations, grey areas where you as a consumer can be potentially misled without the right knowledge. Based on my experience and insider industry insights, it is my goal to help build on your knowledge and empower you to make more healthful and informed choices.

CHAPTER 2

The Food Label Specialist

REVIEWING FOOD LABELS IS NOT easy work; it takes a detailed eye and a lot of patience. As a food label specialist, I have been reviewing food labels for Canadian grocers, national and international manufacturers, importers, and distributors for nearly a decade. Over the years, I have worked on thousands of food labels and often found myself stuck in the middle, trying to strike a balance between the interests of the food companies to competitively market their products and the guidelines set out in the regulations.

Food label specialists review food labels for compliance with Canadian regulations. They work with food companies to help them ensure that their foods meet required Canadian standards; that all ingredients are permitted in Canada; that nutrition information is accurate and displayed correctly; and that claims, images, and additional information are truthful and not misleading. In some cases, food lawyers assist companies with food label reviews, though in such a specialized field, food label specialists are usually more economical.

The number one priority of food label specialists is to ensure all information on the labels they are reviewing is accurate and compliant with the government's regulations; however, the number one priority of food companies is to sell as much food as possible. Provocative marketing, enticing images, and alluring information all attract consumer attention in the store, which can lead to increased sales. However, such efforts can also potentially mislead consumers.

Food label specialists may work in a variety of areas within the grocery supply chain, including working for the manufacturer, importer, distributor, or other companies, such as food-consulting firms and food-analysis labs. My experience is unique in that I have had an opportunity to work as an employee for one of Canada's leading grocery retailers, one of Canada's largest importers of specialty food products, a food manufacturing company, and one of Canada's largest food labs. I have also run my own food label consulting firm, reviewing a broad array of labels from many national and international importers and manufacturers.

I have travelled as far as Asia and Europe to meet with companies in an effort to ensure their compliance with Canadian regulations, and I have had representatives from overseas companies fly to Canada in hopes that a face-to-face meeting might help them better understand Canadian requirements. Unfortunately, this level of due diligence for food label compliance is not common, and many push the limits either intentionally or through a general lack of understanding.

Although there are general similarities, Canada's regulations for labelling food are different from those found in the United States, Europe, and other countries around the world. Even within Canada, some provinces have implemented additional labelling requirements above and beyond the federal standards. As a result, there is often quite

a bit of confusion on the part of food companies, especially international companies, who may have to declare certain ingredients by different names, or nutrition information using different numbers. It is
easy for Canadian regulations to get lost in translation.

It is not uncommon for international food companies to try to
import food products into Canada that contain ingredients that may
be permitted in their countries but that are not permitted in Canada.
In such instances, the only option for the food company should be to
reformulate their products to remove the prohibited ingredients; however, the cost of reformulation is high, and in most circumstances,
importers want to get their products on our shelves as soon as they
can. I have seen some companies simply declare the prohibited ingredients, crossing their fingers that the CFIA won't notice; eventually
they do get caught. I have even worked with a company who made
the preposterous suggestion to simply remove the ingredient from the
label, even though it was still in the product. Obviously that request
didn't fly while under my watch.

Food labels can be presented to food label specialists for review in
a number of ways. The most comprehensive method is when a completed draft of the food label is accompanied by detailed information,
such as the percentage of each ingredient in the product (called the
product formulation); the nutrition information for the product per 100
grams, which is then revised and calculated on a per serving basis; and
the allergy information for the product, including any cross-contami-
nation risks for the facility the product is manufactured in. The detailed
information is compared with the information printed on the draft of

the label, and revisions are made as necessary. This type of label review is thorough and lends itself to the greatest potential for accuracy.

A less efficient though more common method of review is when a food company simply provides a label for review without any additional information. Such detailed product information may be withheld for confidentiality reasons; however, in many cases the company simply may not have the required information, or they are in such a rush to get the label completed and on grocery shelves that they insist that steps be skipped. Unfortunately, the amount of detail reviewed when product formulations and ingredient specifications are received often uncovers non-compliance issues such as ingredients added to products that are not permitted in Canada, or the amount of additives added to foods exceeding Canadian limits.

 Caution!

Although it seems logical to review the draft version of a food label before it shows up on Canadian grocery shelves, it is not unusual for companies to start selling products with potentially incorrect labels that are reviewed only when the CFIA receives a complaint or has flagged a non-compliance issue, or when a major retailer requests a revision before they agree to carry a product in their store. Some of the labels on Canadian grocery shelves have never been reviewed by an expert, and those that have may not have been reviewed in as detailed a way as you might expect.

Most food companies try to work within the government's rules, but some challenge them, some don't understand them, and some simply disregard them. As a food label specialist, I always ensure the correct information is communicated to the food company; however, as consumers, we are really at the mercy of the food companies to revise their labels appropriately. For this reason, I always advise consumers to read their labels with a grain of salt.

CHAPTER 3

What Is a Processed Food?

WHY SPEND THIRTY MINUTES MAKING mashed potatoes from scratch when you can make instant mashed potatoes in less than sixty seconds? Why go to the effort of washing, peeling, and chopping fruit when you can buy ready-to-eat fruit in a can? Why go to the effort of making sauces from scratch when you can just add water? Prepackaged processed foods dominate our grocery store shelves, and many of us have become victim to their accessibility and convenience.

Knowledge is the key to success. How can you make a change when you don't understand the facts? The first step in being able to make informed choices about which processed foods you purchase is to truly understand what a processed food is.

A simple definition of a processed food is a food that has been changed from its natural state. For example, whole oranges are not considered to be processed, but squeezing them into orange juice and then pasteurizing the juice, or peeling and canning the orange segments, would be considered as processing the food. The act of processing a food product generally results in a reduction of the food's nutritional quality and usually requires the addition of flavours; flavour enhancers; and additives such as colours, preservatives, stabilizers, and emulsifiers, as well as some vitamins and minerals to replenish nutrient losses.

Processing methods such as pasteurization help to kill pathogens, which in turn helps to prevent food-related illnesses. The incorporation of additives, such as preservatives, combined with processing methods, also helps to prolong the shelf life of products, thereby increasing the convenience associated with your being able to safely store the food in your kitchen for days, weeks, months, or even years, as is the case with many canned products. Bread may last for a few weeks before turning mouldy, milk can last for weeks in your fridge, canned fruits and vegetables can sit in your cupboards for years, and cookies and crackers remain crisp and crunchy over time. Processed foods may also be less expensive than their natural counterparts, may taste better, and may even look more appealing.

So how can you identify processed foods in your grocery store? On a large scale, almost every product that is placed in the inner aisles of the grocery store is processed: crackers, cookies, pastas, soft drinks, juices, soups, canned vegetables, canned fruit, cereals, salad dressings, jams, etc., leaving the outer aisles mostly for fresh produce, meat, eggs, and dairy products.

Unprocessed foods generally spoil quickly, can be more expensive, and don't always provide the convenience that most of us depend on in our hectic lives. You may not be able to keep a fresh peach in your desk for more than a couple of days, but canned peaches may last for a year or more as an emergency snack.

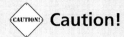 **Caution!**

Although the outside perimeter of the grocery store is where you find fresh fruits and vegetables, meats, and eggs, there is a wide variety of processed foods that can also be found around the perimeter, such as processed frozen foods, processed meats, processed cheeses, processed dairy products, processed fish, and processed bread and bakery products.

I don't want you to feel guilty about eating processed foods; we all do it, myself included. It is important, however, to recognize that not all processed foods are created equally. Some may contain one or two safe additives and may still be beneficial to health, whereas others may contain additives that are potentially hazardous and contribute to disease, along with high levels of fat, sugar, and sodium, and low or insignificant levels of fibre, vitamins, and minerals. It is our responsibility as consumers to identify misleading labels that attempt to trick us into believing that the processed foods we consume are more healthful for us than they really are.

Part 2

An Insider's Perspective on How to Read Food Labels

CHAPTER 4

Food Label Basics

Key Components of a Food Label

WHEN YOU THINK OF THE INFORMATION that is displayed on prepackaged processed food labels, what comes to mind? If you said the nutrition facts table and the list of ingredients, you are not alone. These two elements of the food label are arguably two of the most important, the most read, and the least understood pieces of information.

They are not, however, the only two elements of the prepackaged processed food label that are regulated. Although some information is mandatory and must appear on food labels by law, whereas other information is purely optional, all information on food labels must meet Canadian standards, down to the finest details, including the minimum font size of each letter and number. There are also regulations for bilingual requirements for processed food sold in Canada, including a stipulation that the English and French texts have to be equally prominent (e.g., they must be the same size and colour).

Excluding bilingual requirements, I have broken down the major components of a prepackaged processed food label into the following ten elements. The first five elements are required by law to be shown on *all* prepackaged processed food labels. The second five elements are found on *most* prepackaged processed food labels and may or may not be optional, depending on the type of product. Let's take a closer look …

Five key elements that you will find on all Canadian prepackaged processed food labels:

1. Product Name
2. Net Quantity Statement
3. List of Ingredients
4. Nutrition Facts Table
5. Dealer Name and Address

The additional five elements found on most Canadian prepackaged processed food labels:

1. Brand Name/Logo
2. Claims
3. Romance Text
4. Country-of-Origin Statement (optional with exceptions)
5. Artwork/Graphics

The following are basic descriptions for each of the ten food label elements. The following chapters will go into more detail about how these different elements can potentially mislead consumers. I recommend that you use the definitions in this chapter as a reference for clarification of the terms or definitions used later on. Look for each of these ten elements when reviewing food labels on your own, and keep in mind that each should be read with a grain of salt.

Five Key Elements Found on *All* Prepackaged Processed Food Labels

1. **Product Name**

   The name of the product must appear on the front of the package. Some product names are regulated and represent standardized products, such as milk, cheese, jam, bread, and ice cream; however, many product names are not regulated and are declared by a name that is generally understood by consumers, such as crackers, cookies, and candy. Product descriptions can also accompany product names and may include descriptive information, such as highlighting the main flavour.

   Examples:
   - Product name: cookie
   - Product description: chocolate chip

2. **Net Quantity Statement**

   The net quantity statement (*net weight* or *net volume*) appears on the front of the package. The net quantity allows you to compare the size (amount) of two products more accurately. All things being equal, if two products have the same net quantity, the one with the lower price would be the better value. The net quantity also helps you calculate the nutritional information for the full package versus the serving size given in the nutrition facts table.

   Examples:
   - Net weight: 500 g
   - Net volume: 500 mL

3. **List of Ingredients (including applicable allergen statements)**
   The list of ingredients can be displayed on any panel of the label, including the front, back, or side of the package, but excluding the bottom. Based on the product formulation (recipe), the ingredients used to make the food are listed in descending order by weight.[1] Therefore, the heaviest ingredient (greatest total amount) is listed first, and the lightest ingredient (least amount) is listed last. Some of the ingredients may have their own component ingredients (sub-component ingredients) that may or may not be declared, depending on the type, and possibly the amount, of the ingredient that is found in a product. Ingredients that are present in very small amounts (typically additives, spices, seasonings, herbs, flavours, flavour enhancers, vitamins, and minerals) can be grouped together at the end of the list of ingredients in no particular order.[2]

   Allergens are either clearly labelled within the list of ingredients, or they may be declared in an allergen statement starting with the word "Contains," and possibly "May contain," immediately after the list of ingredients. Note that the "May contain" statement for allergens is optional, so it may not always be present.
   Example:
   - Ingredients: flour, sugar, butter, liquid whole egg
     Contains wheat, milk, and eggs
     May contain soy

---

1 Department of Justice Canada. *Food and Drugs Act.* "Food and Drug Regulations," B.01.008(3).
2 Department of Justice Canada. *Food and Drugs Act.* "Food and Drug Regulations," B.01.008(4).

4. Nutrition Facts Table

In Canada, nutrition facts tables are mandated by law for almost all prepackaged processed food products and may be displayed on any label panel, including the front, back, side, or bottom of the package. The nutrition facts table provides a standard format for listing the suggested serving size, calories, thirteen core nutrients, and the corresponding per cent daily values for most of the core nutrients.

Nutrition Facts Valeur nutritive	
Per 1 can (350 mL) pour 1 canette (350 mL)	
Amount Teneur	% Daily Value % valeur quotidienne
Calories / Calories 130	
Fat / Lipides 1.5 g	2 %
Saturated / saturés 1 g + Trans / trans 0 g	5 %
Cholesterol / Cholestérol 0 mg	
Sodium / Sodium 55 mg	2 %
Carbohydrate / Glucides 29 g	10 %
Fibre / Fibres 0 g	0 %
Sugars / Sucres 26 g	
Protein / Protéines 0 g	
Vitamin A / Vitamine A	0 %
Vitamin C / Vitamine C	20 %
Calcium / Calcium	4 %
Iron / Fer	2 %

5. Dealer Name and Address

It is mandatory for the name and address of the manufacturer, importer, or distributor to appear on any panel of the label, including the front, back, or side of the package, but excluding the bottom. By law, this information must appear on labels so that consumers are able to contact companies with questions, comments, or complaints.

You may wish to use the dealer name and address information if you are concerned with any of the following:

- Allergens: If you are concerned that a product may have come into contact with an allergen or may contain an allergen that is not declared.
- Origin of ingredients: If you would like to try to obtain information on the country of origin of the ingredients in the product.
- Quality: If the quality of the product was wonderful or horrible.

Additional Five Elements Found on
Most Prepackaged Processed Food Labels

6. Brand Name/Logo

   The brand name is a name given by a company to distinguish its products from its competitors. The brand name is generally a registered trademark and usually appears only in English. The brand name is typically accompanied by a company logo, which helps consumers recognize brands at a quick glance.

7. Claims

   Claims are various statements made by food companies that highlight the desirable features of their products. They may be placed in a variety of different places on the package in an effort to catch your eye. Most claims are regulated, though there are a number of "grey areas" and subtleties in meanings.
   Examples:
     - "Made with Whole Grains"
     - "Fat-Free"
     - "Home-Style"

- "A Healthy Diet Low in Saturated and Trans Fats May Reduce the Risk of Heart Disease. Brand X Cookies Are Free of Saturated and Trans Fats."
- "0.2 g Fat per 30 g Serving"

8. **Romance Text**

   Romance text (label copy) is displayed on labels to help marketers convey a story about their brand, company, ingredients, or product. This can be one of the most subtle sources of misleading information on labels.

   Example:

   - "Our bread is baked fresh daily using only the finest ingredients, resulting in a soft, delicious bread that tastes just like homemade."

9. **Country-of-Origin Statement**

   The country-of-origin statement can be found on any panel of the label, including the front, back, or side of the package, but excluding the bottom. It is optional (with exceptions), but it is often included as a result of consumer demand.

   Examples:

   - "Product of Canada"
   - "Product of China"

10. **Artwork/Graphics**

    Not to be overlooked, the artwork, images, and other graphics are important visual cues that consumers use to select their products of choice. Although images must reflect the food that is actually in the package, it is not uncommon for food companies to display images that push the limits of accuracy, perhaps creating an image of the food that is more healthful and enticing than reality.

Now that you have a better understanding of the roles of the food company, food label specialist, and the CFIA, as well as the ten elements of prepackaged processed food labels, let's take a look at the top ways food labels can mislead you from an insider's perspective. The following chapters are designed to help you understand the information and misinformation on food labels and how to avoid being misled.

CHAPTER 5

Brand Names

IF YOU WERE COMPARING TWO CANS of soup in the grocery store, and one had a bright logo above the name "Tomato Soup" that read "Healthy Bowl," and the other simply had a non-specific brand name, which would you find more appealing, and which would you believe was more healthful? If you were comparing two cans of vegetables, and one had a logo above the name "Green Beans" that read "Naturally Divine," and the other simply had a company name, which would you believe was the better-quality product? Get the point?

I created the names above myself, but these scenarios are not uncommon in today's market. Food companies will do everything they can to come up with brand names that not only help to distinguish their products from their competitors but also communicate a variety of potential positive product attributes to further entice consumers.

Although the rules and regulations set out by Health Canada and enforced by the CFIA clearly state that the information displayed on food labels must be truthful and not misleading or deceptive,[1] food

---

1 Canadian Food Inspection Agency. *Guide to Food Labelling and Advertising*, Section 2.2.

companies continually push the limits by incorporating enticing buzz-words such as *healthy, smart, real, choice, fresh,* and *natural* into their brand and trademarked names. If you are to read food labels like an insider, it is important to be aware of some of the tricks of the trade so that you are not easily swayed by these made-up marketing names.

 Did you know?

Trademarked names are usually followed by the trademark symbol (™) or the registered symbol (®).

The Grey Areas: How Food Companies Bend the Rules

There is a general perception in the food industry that because brand and trademarked names and statements are owned by the food companies, they do not have to meet requirements for claims pertaining to any of the words used. Although this is not always the case, the requirements for the use of enticing and suggestive buzzwords in brand names are vague, and thus some food companies take advantage of the grey areas.

Although the CFIA deems the word *natural* to be a claim when incorporated into a trademark name, there is still a lot of ambiguity around the use of buzzwords such as *fresh, real,* and *healthy,* thereby creating the potential for consumers to be misled.

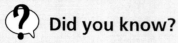 **Did you know?**

The CFIA's *Guide to Food Labelling and Advertising* states that the following requirements must be met to make the claim "Natural" or to incorporate the word *natural* into a trademark or brand name:

"Foods or ingredients of foods submitted to processes that have significantly altered their original physical, chemical or biological state should not be described as 'natural.' This includes such changes as the removal of caffeine.

- A natural food or ingredient of a food is not expected to contain, or to ever have contained, an *added* vitamin, *added* mineral nutrient, artificial flavouring agent or food additive.
- A natural food or ingredient of a food does not have any constituent or fraction thereof *removed* or significantly changed, except the removal of water."*

* Canadian Food Inspection Agency. *Guide to Food Labelling and Advertising*, Section 4.7.

From a regulatory standpoint, the word *fresh*, for example, can be used as part of a trademark name only as long as it is used "in such a manner that it remains clear to the consumer that 'fresh' is not a characteristic of the product and that the name represents a brand."[2] The "grey area" here is in guessing whether the consumer is able to distinguish between the brand name and the product. My guess would be that when the average consumer sees the word *fresh* on a label, the first thing that comes to mind would be that the food in the package is fresh. Whether the word is part of a claim, brand name, or trademarked name, I believe it will almost always be interpreted as a product attribute. The food companies know this, so they try their best to continually incorporate the word *fresh* into their messaging.

The word *real* should not be used to describe foods or ingredients that are imitations or substitutions, nor should it be a used to suggest that a product is entirely real.[3]

With the exception of obvious imitation or substitution products and ingredients (e.g., soy-based cheese, imitation crabmeat, salt substitute), in essence, just about any processed food could be considered at least partially real, and thus food companies can arguably incorporate the word *real* into their brand or trademarked names and statements. Real products should contain at least some ingredients that are real; however, they may also contain some synthetic ingredients. My personal rule of thumb is to never consider prepackaged

---

2 Canadian Food Inspection Agency. *Guide to Food Labelling and Advertising*, Section 4.5.4.
3 Canadian Food Inspection Agency. *Guide to Food Labelling and Advertising*, Section 4.12.

processed foods as natural, or real, because even when they contain only natural ingredients, they have still been manipulated in some way to change them from their raw, natural states.

 Caution!

The word *real* typically refers to natural foods versus synthetic foods. It does not, however, always mean that ingredients have been added to a product in their raw, natural state. Look out for claims such as "Contains Real Fruit" on products that actually contain dehydrated fruits and fruit juices, or "Contains Real Vegetables" on products that actually contain the freeze-dried version. Although these ingredients may be derived from real ingredients, they may not offer the same nutritional benefits as their raw, natural counterparts.

Finally, it is virtually impossible to legitimately incorporate the word *healthy* into brand names, trademarked statements, romance text, or claims on labels. I always discourage food companies from displaying this word because a criterion for the use of the word *healthy*, as it relates to one prepackaged processed food, has yet to be developed by Health Canada, and, therefore, it can always be argued that this claim is misleading. It is also important to note that we all have different nutrient requirements, health conditions, and potential intolerances; therefore, even if a food company legitimately stands behind their product as being "healthy," it may not be a healthful product for you.

It is my understanding that Health Canada recognizes that the increase of implied health claims expressed in commercial logos, symbols, and trademarks is creating confusion in the marketplace; however, their realization may be too little, too late, as new misleading products are popping up every day, and stricter regulations have yet to be developed to deal with this issue.

 Caution!

Look out for trademarked words that are intentially spelled incorrectly, or perhaps shortened, that may appear as the full word to an untrained eye. Derivitives of words such as *antioxidant* and *immune* that have been changed slightly and trademarked are appearing on food labels. They often appear in large, bold, colourful fonts and are placed on the front of food labels to attract shoppers who do not have time to stop and realize the words are actually meaningless.

Although the CFIA includes the following statement in the *Guide to Food Labelling and Advertising* that should prevent food companies from manipulating desirable words that imply health benefits: "Any trademark, brand name, logo or slogan that suggests or implies a health benefit by any means, including through nuance, double meanings, or implied meanings, is generally considered a health claim,"* in reality, these products are out there, and it is up to you as a consumer not to be misled. There is nothing more frustrating than getting home and realizing that what you thought was a juice rich in antioxidants was really a watered-down sweetened version, void of any health-promoting vitamins.

* Canadian Food Inspection Agency. *Guide to Food Labelling and Advertising*, Section 8.2.1.

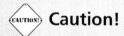 ## Caution!

More and more health-based trademarks (logos, icons, seals of approval, and check marks) are appearing on food labels as food companies try to make their products appear to be "certified as healthy," and thus make shopping easier and quicker. Many consumers, however, find that these unregulated logos actually add to their confusion when shopping.

Requirements to display such icons are made up by the food companies themselves, and not by Health Canada. If you have questions about what qualifies a food to display a specific logo, try contacting the food company for an explanation or check out their website for more information.

Empower Yourself!

1. Look out for potentially misleading trademarked names and statements in Canadian grocery stores that incorporate buzzwords such as *healthy, smart, real, choice, fresh,* and *natural*. Many may represent great products, but be aware that these brand names are purely made up by the food companies, and thus do not guarantee that the food in the package is actually healthful, natural, or smart.

2. Always check the nutrition facts table and list of ingredients when reading labels to determine if the food meets your own personal criteria for healthful and smart.

CHAPTER 6

Product Names

YOU ARE IN THE JAM SECTION OF THE grocery store looking to buy straw-berry jam. Two products catch your eye: one named "Strawberry Jam" and one named "Strawberry Fruit Spread." Both have appealing pictures of juicy strawberries on their labels, and both look as delicious as Grandma's homemade jam. Which one should you buy?

The product name is the name that appears on the front of labels that tells you what is inside the package. Many foods must use *stan-dardized* product names such as Cheddar cheese, ice cream, and jam. These names have been defined by Health Canada and have rules and regulations attached to them. Slightly modified standardized foods may use what are called *modified common names*, and other foods, known as *unstandardized* foods, that do not have to meet specific requirements (with the exception of additives), simply use the name by which the food is generally known; for example, cookies, crackers, and candy.

The Grey Areas: How Food Companies Bend the Rules

Foods that must use specific product names are called *standardized foods*. The ingredients that manufacturers are allowed to add to these foods are all laid out in the regulations, and food companies must use the exact name prescribed in the regulations if the product meets the standard. There is a long list of standardized foods, and, in essence, all other foods are considered to be modified or unstandardized, or for the purposes of this book, "imposter products."

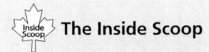

The Inside Scoop

Visit the "Inside Scoop" page at www.grainofsalt.ca and type in the password KNOWLEDGE to gain access. Under the "Product Names" section look for the list of standardized product names as per the *Food and Drugs Act*, "Food and Drug Regulations," Part B.

Let's consider the strawberry jam example above. To call a product "Strawberry Jam," it must contain a minimum of 45 per cent fruit (in this case, strawberries) and may contain pectin, a preservative, a pH adjusting agent, and an antifoaming agent, and it may not contain apple or rhubarb.[1] If a strawberry jam contained less than 45 per cent strawberries, or contained two or more preservatives, its name would no longer be permitted to incorporate the word *jam*.

The addition or removal of just one ingredient can change a product name entirely, and at a glance may not be noticeable to the average consumer. Even worse, without comparing lists of ingredients, you may not know which product name applies to the higher-quality product. You may get tricked into buying "Strawberry Fruit Spread" with potentially far less fruit and far more sugar and additives (it may look like Grandma's jam, but it certainly won't taste like it).

---

1. Department of Justice Canada. *Food and Drugs Act.* "Food and Drug Regulations," B.11.201. [S].

Let's consider another example: "Apple Juice" (a standardized product) versus "Apple Drink" (an imposter product). Both may contain juice from apples, but the "Apple Drink" has lost its "juice" status as it does not meet the requirements for the amount of juice it must contain, or it may contain other ingredients that are not permitted in the standardized product. Whereas apple juice must be juice obtained solely from apples, apple drink is most likely flavoured sugar water trying to imitate apple juice.

Here is an example of a list of ingredients for apple juice:

• Ingredients: 100% apple juice.

And here is an example of a list of ingredients for apple drink:

• Ingredients: water, sugar/glucose-fructose, concentrated fruit juices (apple and/or grape and/or pear), malic acid, natural and artificial flavours, sodium citrate, ascorbic acid (vitamin C), colour.

If you know the difference between the product names "Apple Juice" and "Apple Drink," which intentionally sound very similar, you should be able to avoid purchasing the imposter when you are looking for the real deal.

 Did you know?

Drinks that contain at least 25 per cent of a single juice may incorporate the name of the juice into the product's name.* For example, if apple juice were present in an amount of at least 25 per cent in the

"Apple Drink" example, the name of the beverage could change to "Apple Juice Drink," creating another level of complexity to label reading. The percentage of juice present should also appear on the front of the label, but it is not always incorporated into the name of the product, which means you may not notice the information.

When the percentage of juice is less than 25 per cent, the word *juice* cannot appear as part of the name of the product; however, the statement "Made with XX% Fruit Juice" would still be permitted to appear on the label.[†]

Also, be aware that claims such as "Has the Taste of Freshly Squeezed Orange Juice" are allowed to appear on drink products that may not contain any real juice at all.[†] Always read the list of ingredients to determine what you are buying.

* Canadian Food Inspection Agency. *Guide to Food Labelling and Advertising*, Section 9.6.1.

† Ibid.

Another great example is chocolate. Chocolate is one of my favourite foods, and I know that I'm not alone. When I eat chocolate, I want it to melt in my mouth and taste rich, creamy, and smooth. It used to baffle me that some chocolate bars cost upwards of $5, when others cost less than a dollar, but now I know such a price difference may be due not only to a significant variance in the quality of certain chocolates, but also to the fact that many of the inexpensive chocolate bars are not made with real chocolate at all.

Milk chocolate is one of the most popular types of chocolate, and my favourite, so let's take milk chocolate as an example. For a product to be called "Milk Chocolate" or to be referred to as containing milk chocolate, it must –

- contain one or more of the following: "cocoa liquor," "cocoa liquor and cocoa butter," or "cocoa butter and cocoa powder" combined with a sweetening ingredient;
- not contain less than 25 per cent total cocoa solids, of which not less than 15 per cent is cocoa butter and not less than 2.5 per cent is fat-free cocoa solids; and
- not contain less than 12 per cent total milk solids from milk ingredients, and it cannot contain less than 3.39 per cent milk fat.[2]

Although this may not mean much to you, what you should know is that these specifications are what makes rich, creamy, delicious milk chocolate.

Cocoa liquor and cocoa butter are the essence of good chocolate and cost much more than cocoa. Many food companies develop products that simply contain cocoa and a handful of additives that make a product appear and taste as similar to chocolate as possible. If your chocolate bar or chocolate coating tastes waxy and artificial, more than

2 Department of Justice Canada. *Food and Drugs Act.* "Food and Drug Regulations," B.04.008. [S].

likely it is because it is an imposter product!

Although companies are not allowed to call products "Chocolate" that contain only cocoa, or do not meet the requirements for chocolate products, as defined in the Food and Drug Regulations, they are allowed to call these (imposter) products "Chocolaty," "Chocolate Flavoured," or "Chocolate-Like."[3] Although these names may look and sound similar to the word *chocolate*, don't be fooled!

Here is a typical list of ingredients for a real milk chocolate bar:

- Ingredients: sugar, whole milk powder, cocoa liquor, cocoa butter, soy lecithin, vanilla extract.

And here is an example of a possible list of ingredients for a chocolaty or chocolate-flavoured bar:

- Ingredients: sugar, modified milk ingredients, cocoa, soy lecithin, artificial flavour, colour, salt, potassium sorbate.

Chocolate labelling becomes a little messy with foods such as chocolate pudding, chocolate cake, chocolate frosting, chocolate cookies, and chocolate cake mixes, which can still incorporate the word *chocolate* into their names to describe the flavour of the food, when in fact they may not contain real chocolate at all.[4] It is believed that these products are not usually mistaken for containing real chocolate; however, when I make most of these foods from scratch, I use real chocolate.

The following is a list of ingredients for a milk chocolate pudding product. Although it contains cocoa, it is far from the real deal.

---

3 Canadian Food Inspection Agency. *Guide to Food Labelling and Advertising*, Section 9.3.
4 Ibid.

- Ingredients: skim milk from concentrate (water, concentrated skim milk), sugar, water, hydrogenated soybean oil, modified corn starch, cocoa, salt, coffee powder, sodium stearoyl-2-lactylate, vanilla extract.

The use of the word *fudge* further complicates the issue. This word does not have to meet any standards (with the exception of additives) and, in my opinion, implies that the food is far from anything that ever resembled chocolate. For some reason, though, I always picture the dark, gooey, fudgy icing on ice cream cakes, and I find the word appealing. Do not be misled; this word is typically used for low-quality foods that are trying their hardest to resemble superior products.

Moving on, let's look at another popular example of an imposter product. "Ice Cream" versus "Frozen Dairy Dessert" is one of my favourite misleading product-name phenomena. When you think of ice cream, what do you imagine? Frozen cream and sugar combined with berries, chocolate, or another natural sweet and delicious ingredient?

This is the most appealing prepackaged ice cream list of ingredients I have come across:

Vanilla Ice Cream:

- Ingredients: cream, skim milk, sugar, liquid egg yolk, natural vanilla extract.

Sounds delicious, and because the product is called "Ice Cream" (a standardized product name), you know that it was made with cream, milk, or milk products that have been combined with sweetening ingredients, such as sugar, and other potential optional ingredients that are permitted in the regulation.[5]

The problem food companies have with making real ice cream is that fresh cream and milk ingredients are relatively expensive. It is much more cost-efficient for them to use water and modified milk ingredients combined with additives to produce a product that resembles ice cream. Synthetic-tasting soft-serve ice cream always comes to mind, but now grocery store shelves are laden with imposter ice cream products disguised in ice cream containers and boxes that are being called "Frozen Dairy Desserts."

One of the main contributing factors to the frozen dairy dessert phenomenon is the fat-free craze. When fat is removed from a product, the ingredients (product formulation) are almost always changed to compensate for the loss of flavour, texture, and mouth feel. In the case of ice cream, when the cream and milk are removed, you are really just left with ice and sugar, thus additives are added into the food to substitute for the fat that has been removed, thereby increasing palatability (taste and texture). Here is the result:

Frozen Dairy Dessert example:

- Ingredients: milk ingredients, modified milk ingredients, sugar/glucose-fructose, polydextrose, maltodextrin, water, artificial flavour, propylene glycol mono fatty acid esters, mono- and diglycerides, cellulose gum, carob bean gum, guar gum, carrageenan, sodium benzoate.

---

5 Department of Justice Canada. *Food and Drugs Act.* "Food and Drug Regulations," B.08.062. [S].

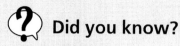 Did you know?

The ingredient "milk ingredients" can be any one or a combination of the following ingredients in liquid, concentrated, dry, frozen, or reconstituted form:*

1. Milk

2. Skim milk

3. Partly skimmed milk

4. Butter

5. Cream

6. Buttermilk

7. Butter oil

8. Milk fat

9. Any other component of milk, the chemical composition of which has not been altered and that exists in the food in the same chemical state in which it is found in milk

Milk ingredients can be labelled by their actual names (i.e., "milk," "skim milk," "cream," etc.) as indicated above, or they can be grouped together and labelled as "milk ingredients." Wholesome ingredients like milk and cream are high-quality superior ingredients that consumers like to see listed in the list of ingredients; therefore, if you see the ingredient "milk ingredients" declared, it is generally safe to assume that that the product contains the lower-quality ingredients, such as milk powder and reconstituted milk.

* Department of Justice Canada. *Food and Drugs Act.* "Food and Drug Regulations," B.01.010(3)(b)(7).

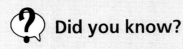 Did you know?

"Modified milk ingredients" may include any of the following in liquid, concentrated, dry, frozen, or reconstituted form:*

1. Calcium-reduced skim milk (obtained by the ion-exchange process)

2. Casein

3. Caseinates

4. Cultured milk products

5. Milk serum proteins

6. Ultrafiltered milk

7. Whey

8. Whey butter

9. Whey cream

10. Any other component of milk in which the chemical state has been altered from that in which it is found in milk

* Department of Justice Canada. *Food and Drugs Act.* "Food and Drug Regulations," B.01.010(3)(b)(7.1).

 Caution!

1. Always look for the real deal first in the list of ingredients. If a product should typically contain real milk or real cream, is it listed?

2. Consider products that list "milk ingredients" instead of the actual name of the milk product. Remember that the chemical

composition of these ingredients has not been altered, but they may be present in the product in a lower-quality form (i.e., dry, frozen, or reconstituted).

3. Be skeptical when considering products that list "modified milk ingredients." Remember that their chemical state has been altered from that found in milk. Although the word *milk* appears as part of the ingredient name, these ingredients are far from wholesome milk.

Empower Yourself!

1. Look out for imposter names that closely resemble traditional food names (standardized products). If something doesn't look quite right to you, it is probably because it isn't. Read the list of ingredients to make sure you understand the composition of the product.

2. Remember that food companies are not permitted to display a product name on a label that may mislead a consumer into thinking they are purchasing a different, more healthful, or better-quality product than what is actually in the package. Keep in mind, however, that this does not mean that food companies do not try their best to convince you otherwise. Imposter names on food labels are one of the areas where a food company's marketers' talents really shine, and it is up to you as a consumer to read these names with a grain of salt.

 **Did you know?**

A slight change in the formulation (recipe of ingredients) of a standardized food may deem it necessary to change the product name from that found in the Food and Drug Regulations. Watch out for the following ten imposter product names, which to the untrained eye can be misleading:

1. "Maple Syrup" may change to "Maple-Flavoured Syrup" or "Table Syrup"
2. "Ice Cream" may change to "Frozen Dairy Dessert"
3. "Chocolate" may change to "Chocolaty," "Chocolate Flavoured," or "Chocolate-Like"
4. "Strawberry Jam" may change to "Strawberry Spread"
5. "Apple Sauce" may change to "Apple Snack"
6. "Mayonnaise" may change to "Dressing Sauce" or "Whipped Dressing"
7. "Processed Cheese" may change to "Processed Cheese Product"
8. "Orange Juice" may change to "Orange Drink"
9. "Apple Juice" may change to "Apple Juice Beverage"
10. "Whipped Cream"* may change to "Dessert Topping"

* Note that although the food "whipped cream" does not have a standard prescribed in the Food and Drug Regulations, many imposter whipped cream products on the market do not contain cream at all.

CHAPTER 7

Ingredients Hidden in Class Names

IN MY OPINION, THE LIST OF INGREDIENTS is the most important piece of information on food labels. Some may argue the nutrition information is more important, but as the saying goes, "We are what we eat," and the list of ingredients is where we are able to find out what we are eating.

As a rule, based on the product formulation (recipe), the ingredients used to make the food are listed in descending order by weight.[1] Therefore, the heaviest ingredient (greatest total amount by weight) is listed first, and the lightest ingredient (least amount by weight) is listed last. Keep in mind, however, that the ingredients that many of us are the most concerned about, such as flavour enhancers and food additives (including preservatives), can be listed in any order at the end of the list of ingredients, regardless of weight.[2]

---

1 Department of Justice Canada. *Food and Drugs Act.* "Food and Drug Regulations," B.01.008(3).
2 Department of Justice Canada. *Food and Drugs Act.* "Food and Drug Regulations," B.01.008(4).

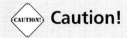 **Caution!**

Just because you see additives listed at the end of the list of ingredients does not always mean they are present in the product in the least amount.

In my experience, I would say that the majority of prepackaged processed foods list their ingredients in a truthful manner that is typically not misleading; however, there are varying degrees of "grey areas" and even some loopholes in the regulations that can not only potentially mislead consumers but also perhaps trick them into believing they are purchasing a product that is more healthful than it is in reality.

The Grey Areas: How Food Companies Bend the Rules

There are two main ways food companies can hide ingredients on food labels. The first is by using an approved class name for an ingredient, and the second is by taking advantage of an exemption that allows for certain ingredients/categories of ingredients (there are approximately fifty of them) to not declare their subcomponents when found as an ingredient in prepackaged foods.

Let's start with class names for ingredients: There are twenty-four defined class names for ingredients that allow companies to declare one or more similar ingredients under one ingredient name. Although not typical, you could have upwards of ten different ingredients declared on a label as one ingredient name, and it is definitely not far fetched to find three to five ingredients declared under one class name. Class names make the list of ingredients easier to read but, in my opinion, often more difficult to understand.

Class names for ingredients are typically used by the food industry for the following reasons:

- They help to shorten the list of ingredients, which may be necessary on small packages that do not have a lot of room for label information.
- They protect food companies from having to disclose proprietary product formulation information, which allows them to remain competitive in their market.
- They allow manufacturers some flexibility when sourcing similar ingredients from different suppliers without having to update their labels.
- They help to make the list of ingredients appear more appealing to consumers. Would you rather buy a product that declares the ingredient "colour," or a product that declares the ingredient "brilliant blue FCF"? How about "sulphites" versus "sulphurous acid"? I think the choices are obvious.

Consumers are at a major disadvantage when ingredients are labelled using class names for two reasons:

1. They do not always understand what the ingredient class names mean (i.e., which ingredients can be grouped together under a specific class name).
2. They do not know exactly what they are eating (i.e., although they may understand which ingredients can be grouped

together under a specific class name, they do not know which of the hidden ingredients are specifically in the product they are considering).

Let's look at an example. There are currently thirty-five colours permitted in foods in Canada. Of those thirty-five, ten are artificial and twenty-five are natural.[3] If a product contains one colour or upwards of thirty colours, they can simply be declared as "colour" in the list of ingredients. It is not necessary to include an indication as to whether the colours contained in the product are natural or artificial. From a consumer's perspective, it is virtually impossible to determine if a product contains natural colours, artificial colours, or a mixture of the two unless the claim "No Artificial Colours" appears on the label. At one point a few years ago, I was actually discouraged by the CFIA from declaring the ingredient name "natural colour" on a label for a product that contained only natural colours; however, now this ingredient name seems to be popping up more and more.

If you were to compare lists of ingredients for the following two identical candy products, which would you buy?

Candy product A:

• Ingredients: sugar, natural flavour, colour.

Candy product B:

• Ingredients: sugar, natural flavour, sunset yellow FCF, allura red, brilliant blue FCF.

---

3 Department of Justice Canada. *Food and Drugs Act.* "Food and Drug Regulations," Division 16, Table III.

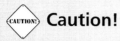 **Caution!**

Vegans beware! Cochineal is a natural colour extracted from dried and crushed female cochineal beetles. The colour is typically red (may include different shades of red and orange) and is permitted in many foods in Canada, such as jams, flavoured milks, baked goods, and cheese.* In my ten years of working as a food label specialist, I have never once labelled this ingredient by its actual name cochineal, nor have I ever read a food label that has labelled this colour as "cochineal." Although Canada allows this ingredient to be labelled under the class name "colour," as of January 5, 2011, the colour cochineal extract must be labelled by its actual name on all food labels in the United States.† Maybe it's time for Canada to follow suit?

* Department of Justice Canada. *Food and Drugs Act.* "Food and Drug Regulations," Division 16, Table III.

† US Food and Drug Administration. *Laws, Regulations and Guidance.* "Guidance for Industry: Cochineal Extract and Carmine: Declaration by Name on the Label of All Foods and Cosmetic Products That Contain These Color Additives: Small Entity Compliance Guide." April 2009.

Here is another less alarming example: The ingredient name "vinegar" can be used for eight different types of vinegar. The food could actually contain one, all eight, or any number of the following types of vinegar: wine vinegar, spirit vinegar, alcohol vinegar, white vinegar, grain vinegar, malt vinegar, cider vinegar, or apple vinegar.[4] Before

4 Department of Justice Canada. *Food and Drugs Act.* "Food and Drug Regulations," B.01.010(3)(b)(23).

starting my career, I thought the ingredient "vinegar" always referred to white vinegar, but now I know better.

Another way class ingredients can be misleading on labels is when food companies break up a class ingredient in order to manipulate the order of ingredients so that superior ingredients are declared closer to the top of the list of ingredients. As ingredients are always declared in descending order by weight, it is often advantageous for a food company to declare the more healthful, most natural, and highest-quality ingredients first.

Let's look at a raspberry jam example. Many of the best jams on the market contain more fruit than sugar. In essence, jam is really just a mixture of fruit and sugar with a few additives to help thicken it and keep it from spoiling. Therefore, it is generally understood that jams that list the fruit component first in the list of ingredients are potentially a better buy than jams that list sugar as the first ingredient, but as you can see here, this is not always the case.

Jam #1 displays the following list of ingredients:

- Ingredients: raspberries, **liquid sugar**, **sugar**, concentrated lemon juice, pectin.

Jam #2 displays the following list of ingredients:

- Ingredients: **sugar**, raspberries, concentrated lemon juice, pectin.

Although jam #1 appears to be a higher-quality product, it is important to note that the company has not used the class name "sugar" to declare the sugar ingredients found in the product. It is possible that if the weights of the ingredients "liquid sugar" and "sugar" were combined, they could weigh more than the raspberries and would have to be declared first, similar to jam #2.

Another great example is the manipulation of the labelling of vegetable oils within the list of ingredients to give a false impression that a food contains less fat than it actually does. Vegetable oil is an approved class name that, when used as an ingredient name, actually means a combination of one or more different types of oil derived from plants such as olives, corn, soybeans, and canola (excluding coconut oil, palm oil, palm kernel oil, peanut oil, or cocoa butter, which must be declared by their actual names[5]). Because we know that ingredients are declared in descending order by weight, many consumers typically look for vegetable oil to be declared as far from the top as possible. The following two virtually identical cookies contain the same amount of fat, but one may appear to be more healthful based on the order of ingredients:

Cookie #1:

- Ingredients: wheat flour, brown sugar, **vegetable oil**, milk, sugar, skim milk powder, dried whole egg, salt, baking soda, natural flavour, baking powder.

Cookie #2:

- Ingredients: wheat flour, brown sugar, milk, sugar, skim milk powder, **canola oil**, dried whole egg, **olive oil**, **corn oil**, salt, baking soda, natural flavour, baking powder.

---

5 Department of Justice Canada. *Food and Drugs Act.* "Food and Drug Regulations," B.01.010(3)(b)(1).

Ingredient Class Names

The following are the twenty-four approved class names for ingredients, along with an explanation of their meanings.[6]

1. Vegetable Oil or Vegetable Fat
   - Contrary to popular belief, "vegetable oil" is not a specific type of oil; it is a combination of one or more different types of oil derived from plants such as olives, corn, soybeans, and canola. The following oils and fats cannot be included in the ingredient class name "vegetable oil" or "vegetable fat" and have to be declared by their actual names: coconut oil, palm oil, palm kernel oil, peanut oil, and cocoa butter.

 Caution!

Do not be misled by vibrant images of fresh vegetables that may appear on some vegetable oil labels. These images are displayed on labels to entice consumers while shopping and are typically not representative of what is actually in the bottle. If you are considering a vegetable oil product, be sure to read the list of ingredients to determine which types of oil the product contains.

---

6 Department of Justice Canada. *Food and Drugs Act.* "Food and Drug Regulations," B.01.010(3)(b)(1–23).

2. Marine Oil
   - The ingredient "marine oil" is not often seen on food labels. In my ten-year career, I have never once labelled an ingredient by this name, probably because it sounds like oil used for a boat engine. However, if you do see it, the ingredient can contain one or more marine fats or oils (i.e., fish).

3. Spices, Seasonings, Herbs
   - The ingredients "spices," "seasonings," and "herbs" are commonly seen in the list of ingredients and are used to describe one or more spices, seasonings, or herbs. If salt is contained in a spice, seasoning, or herb mixture, it cannot be hidden and must be declared by its common name "salt" within the list of ingredients.

 Caution!

The words *seasoning* and *seasoned* do not mean the same thing. The word *seasoning* is typically used to describe an ingredient that contains a mixture of salt, spices, herbs, and, potentially, flavours, whereas the word *seasoned* is used to describe products (usually solid cuts of meat) to which potassium salts, salt, and/or water have been added.*

* Canadian Food Inspection Agency. *Guide to Food Labelling and Advertising*, Section 14.4.2.

4. Bacterial Culture
   - Bacterial cultures are often found in cheese products and are permitted to contain one or more species of bacteria. The actual name of the bacteria probably wouldn't mean much to an average consumer, so this class name makes label reading easier.

5. Mould Culture or Mold Culture
   - Similar to "bacterial culture," "mould culture" is often found in cheese products and is the declaration used to describe one or more species of mould.

6. Rennet
   - Rennet is typically found in cheese products and is the declaration used to describe a preparation containing the enzyme rennin.

7. Microbial Enzyme
   - "Microbial enzyme" is the name given to milk-coagulating enzymes from *Aspergillus oryzae* RET-1 (pBoel777), *Endothia parasitica*, *Mucor miehei*, or *Mucor pusillus Lindt* that are typically found in cheese products. Can you imagine seeing these enzyme names on labels? "Microbial enzyme" doesn't sound as scary, and it is much easier to read.

8. Carbonated Water
   - When carbon dioxide is added to water, it makes carbonated water. The ingredient class name "carbonated water" is, therefore, allowed to be used instead of listing both water and carbon dioxide in the list of ingredients.

9. Water
   - When you see the ingredient name "water" in the list of ingredients, it refers to demineralized water or water that has been treated to remove hardness or impurities, or fluoridated or chlorinated water.

10. Vinegar
    - Just about every type of vinegar can be grouped together and declared as "vinegar" in the list of ingredients, including one or more of the following: wine vinegar, spirit vinegar, alcohol vinegar, white vinegar, grain vinegar, malt vinegar, cider vinegar, or apple vinegar.

11. Toasted Wheat Crumbs
    - If you have ever wondered what toasted wheat crumbs are, here is the answer: Toasted wheat crumbs are made by cooking a dough prepared with flour and water, which may be unleavened or chemically or yeast leavened. Basically, it is bread crumbs with a fancy name, though the quality of bread (number of additives used) is often unknown because they do not have to be declared. A toasted wheat crumbs' list of ingredients could look similar to this if all of the ingredients were declared on the label:
      - Ingredients: wheat flour, yeast, natural flavour, dextrose, wheat gluten, salt, ascorbic acid.

12. Colour
    - Both natural and artificial colours are allowed to be grouped together and declared as "colour" on food labels. The food could contain one natural colour or a combination of many natural and artificial colours, and you would be none the wiser. There

are some exceptions for specific meat products; however, for just about every product on the market that is permitted to contain colour, this is the case.

13. Flavour
  • Natural flavours, or flavours produced from animal or vegetable raw materials, can be grouped together and called "flavour" in the list of ingredients. The good news is that the ingredient "flavour" is allowed to be used only to describe natural flavours. Unlike the regulations for colour, artificial flavours cannot be grouped together with natural flavours and must be declared separately.

14. Name of the Plant or Animal Source plus the Word "Flavour"
  • Natural flavours produced from a plant or animal can also be labelled to include the name of the plant or animal source used to create the flavour. For example, "vanilla flavour," "peppermint flavour," or "strawberry flavour" could be used. This type of declaration is commonly found on foods that highlight the flavour in the name or description of the product. For example, a cereal called "Strawberry-Flavoured Flakes" would most likely include the ingredient name "strawberry flavour" versus just "flavour."

15. Artificial Flavour, Imitation Flavour, or Simulated Flavour
  • Although companies most commonly use the ingredient declaration "artificial flavour," the ingredient names "imitation flavour" and "simulated flavour" mean the same thing. These declarations refer to one or more flavours derived completely or partially by chemical synthesis.

16. Milk Ingredients
    - Milk ingredients include ingredients such as milk, partly skimmed milk, skim milk, butter, buttermilk, butter oil, milk fat, and cream. These ingredients have not had their chemical composition altered; however, they may be included in liquid, concentrated, dry, frozen, or reconstituted form.
17. Modified Milk Ingredients
    - Modified milk ingredients include ingredients such as calcium-reduced skim milk (obtained by the ion-exchange process), casein, caseinates, cultured milk products, milk serum proteins, ultrafiltered milk, whey, whey butter, and whey cream. These ingredients are different from milk ingredients in that their chemical composition has been altered from how they are found in milk. They can also be included in liquid, concentrated, dry, frozen, or reconstituted form.

 Did you know?

The ingredient class name "modified milk ingredients" can be used to describe milk ingredients that have had their chemical composition altered, but it can also be used to describe a combination of milk ingredients and modified milk ingredients.* Unless space is extremely limited on a label, food companies do not typically group milk ingredients that have not been modified with those that have, as this would potentially create an impression that a product is less natural than it really is.

* Department of Justice Canada. *Food and Drugs Act.* "Food and Drug Regulations," B.01.010(3)(b)(7.2).

18. Sodium Phosphate or Sodium Phosphates
    - Any combination of the additives disodium phosphate, monosodium phosphate, sodium hexametaphosphate, sodium tripolyphosphate, tetrasodium pyrophosphate, and sodium acid pyrophosphate can be grouped together in the list of ingredients and simply declared as "sodium phosphate" or "sodium phosphates." Look for the plural, "phosphates," to perhaps indicate that multiple additives are present.

19. Gum Base
    - Gum base is found in chewing gum and is the part that does not impart sweetness, flavour, or colour, not including the coating. Gum base can provide longer-lasting flavour, improved texture, and reduced tackiness; however, in many cases it may be made from synthetic materials, such as rubbers, and may contain preservatives, such as BHA and BHT. I guess we aren't supposed to swallow our gum for good reason!

20. Sulphites, Sulfites, Suphiting Agents, and Sufiting Agents
    - Sulphites or sulphiting agents is the unassuming class name given when one or more of the following preservatives have been added to a food: potassium bisulphite, potassium metabisulphite, sodium bisulphite, sodium dithionite, sodium metabisulphite, sodium sulphite, sulphur dioxide, and sulphurous acid. I'm not sure about you, but if I saw a product with the ingredient "sulphurous acid" declared, I would put it back on the shelf; however, I may be less averse to buying a product that simply listed the ingredient "sulphites." Although sulphites can also be naturally occurring in foods, an ingredient declared

by the class name "sulphites" should almost always be translated to mean "preservatives."

21. Sugar

- When you see the ingredient "sugar" listed on food labels, I'm sure the first thing that comes to mind is white crystallized sugar—the sugar many of us love to add to our coffee, sprinkle on our breakfast cereal, and use in our home baking. The ingredient class name "sugar," however, can actually refer to any combination of sugar, liquid sugar, invert sugar, or liquid invert sugar.

 Caution!

Because "sugar" is both a standardized ingredient name and an optional ingredient class name, it is not uncommon to see the ingredient "sugar" declared separately from ingredients such as "liquid sugar," "invert sugar," or "liquid invert sugar," as seen in the jam list of ingredients example on page 51. When reading the list of ingredients, always look out for multiple sources of sugar (please see chapter 9 for a list of twenty-five common ingredient names for sugar).

22. Fructose Syrup

- The ingredient name "fructose syrup" is used when glucose syrups contain greater than 60 per cent fructose. If you are concerned with the amount of fructose in your diet, look out for this ingredient name.

23. Glucose-Fructose
    • The ingredient name "glucose-fructose" is used for glucose syrups that contain less than 60 per cent fructose. Do not be misled by this ingredient class name; nine times out of ten it is actually high-fructose corn syrup.

24. Sugar/Glucose-Fructose
    • The ingredient name "sugar/glucose-fructose" is typically used when a product contains both sugar and the ingredient glucose-fructose as described above. Again, watch out for this ingredient name if you are concerned about high-fructose corn syrup. Although it is considered one ingredient name, it can actually mean that you are getting a double dose of sugar.

The Inside Scoop

Visit the "Inside Scoop" page at www.grainofsalt.ca and type in the password KNOWLEDGE to gain access. Under the "Ingredients" section, look for the detailed definitions of the above-listed twenty-four class names for ingredients as per the *Food and Drugs Act*, "Food and Drug Regulations," B.01.010(3)(b)(1–23).

Empower Yourself!

1. Keep this list of ingredient class names handy when reading food labels. Remember that vague ingredient names are more than likely composed of one or more ingredients that you may want to avoid. Talk to your health-care provider about why some ingredients may be worth avoiding.

2. When comparing food labels, remember to keep in mind that one product may declare an ingredient by its class name, whereas another product may declare all ingredients in one class by their actual names (i.e., "sugar" versus "sugar and liquid sugar," or "vegetable oil" versus "olive oil and canola oil").

3. Keep in mind that multiple ingredients that are not declared using a class name may be present in a product in the same amount or more compared with a product that does use a class name and declares the ingredient closer to the top of the list of ingredients. Be sure to refer to the nutrition facts table to ensure specific nutrient amounts are within your target ranges.

4. If you are concerned about consuming an ingredient that may be hidden behind an ingredient class name, try contacting the food company to request further information. They may not tell you exactly which ingredients comprise the class of ingredients, but they may be able to tell you if the ingredient you are specifically concerned with is in the product or not.

5. If you are not able to determine which ingredients are hidden behind an ingredient class name, and you are concerned about the product, leave it on the shelf and look for another product that discloses the information you need to feel comfortable.

CHAPTER 8

Hidden Component Ingredients

HAVE YOU EVER BOUGHT A FROZEN CHICKEN breast stuffed with cheese, and the cheese ingredient was simply declared as "Cheddar cheese"? Cheese is always made up of more than one ingredient, so why have these ingredients not been declared? How about a frozen pizza with bacon declared as "bacon"? Almost all bacon contains nitrites, which are a concern to many people, so why haven't they been declared? When component ingredients are hidden in the lists of ingredients of prepackaged processed foods, how can you know what you are really eating?

There are two types of ingredients that can be found in foods:

1. Simple, pure ingredients such as fruits and vegetables.
2. Complex ingredients that are composed of a combination of foods and/or additives such as cheese and preserved meats.

When an ingredient is made up of multiple foods and/or additives, these foods/additives are called *component ingredients*. Component ingredients are typically listed in parentheses after the main ingredient is declared, or within the list of ingredients in descending order by weight.[1] Most companies declare the component ingredients in parentheses after the main ingredient; therefore, you would most likely see Cheddar cheese declared similarly to "Cheddar cheese (milk, bacterial culture, salt, microbial enzyme)." I'm sure this looks familiar!

 Did you know?

Although it is typical to differentiate cheese products based on whether they are what many of us consider to be *natural cheese* versus *processed cheese*, it is important to note that what many of us call *natural cheese* may also contain a handful of additives (including preservatives) that you may wish to avoid.

Processed cheese has long been referred to as *plastic cheese*, and for good reason; it has a strange rubbery texture and sometimes doesn't even have to be refrigerated. (I'm always baffled when I see packages of processed cheese at the end of a grocery aisle on a cardboard display far from the refrigerated section of the store.) Contrary to popular belief, processed cheese does have to contain real cheese (processed cheese food and processed cheese spread must contain no less than 51 per cent cheese*); however, it is different from conventional cheese in that it can also contain water, sweetening agents such as

1 Department of Justice Canada. *Food and Drugs Act.* "Food and Drug Regulations," B.01.008(5).

sugar, emulsifiers, and other additives. There is a reason why processed cheese is less expensive than real cheese—milk costs more than water!

* Department of Justice Canada. *Food and Drugs Act.* "Food and Drug Regulations," B.08.041.1(1). [S] and B.08.041.3(1). [S].

Caution!

If you can't eat a grilled cheese sandwich without a processed cheese slice, consider the following list of different types of processed cheese, listed in order of descending quality:

1. Look for the name "Processed Cheese"; if you can't find this, look for ...

2. "Processed Cheese Food"; if you can't find this, look for ...

3. "Processed Cheese Spread"; if you can't find this, you are left with ...

4. "Processed Cheese Product," an imposter processed cheese that either doesn't meet the minimum or maximum levels defined in Divison 8 of the Food and Drug Regulations for the amount of cheese in the product, the amount of moisture, or the amount of milk fat, or it has additional additives or ingredients added that are not prescribed in the regulations for processed cheese.

There are, however, approximately fifty different ingredients/categories of ingredients where the declaration of their component ingredients is optional and not required by law. This means that if you were to buy a package of Cheddar cheese on its own, its ingredients would be displayed on its label; however, if you bought chicken breasts stuffed with Cheddar cheese, you may only see the ingredient "Cheddar cheese" declared, without its component ingredients. An exception is that food companies still have to declare any major allergens if they are hidden within the component ingredients.

The following is a typical list of ingredients for margarine:

• Ingredients: canola oil, water, modified palm oil, salt, whey powder, soy lecithin, potassium sorbate, mono- and diglycerides, citric acid, alpha-tocopherol acetate, calcium disodium EDTA, natural and artificial flavour, carotene, vitamin A palmitate, vitamin D3.

If the exact list of ingredients as shown above were found in a product such as cookies, it would be permitted to be declared as "margarine (contains soy)," as soy is an allergen. Consider the following two lists of ingredients that illustrate how misleading hiding component ingredients can be:

List of Ingredients A:

• Cookies: flour, sugar, margarine (contains soy), vanilla.

List of Ingredients B:

• Cookies: flour, sugar, margarine (canola oil, water, modified palm oil, salt, whey powder, soy lecithin, potassium sorbate, mono- and diglycerides, citric acid, alpha-tocopherol acetate, calcium disodium EDTA, natural and artificial flavour, carotene, vitamin A palmitate, vitamin D3), vanilla.

The unfortunate reality is that you could be eating preservatives and artificial flavours and not even know it. Food companies typically take advantage of this permitted labelling exemption to not only keep their lists of ingredients shorter but also to remain competitive. If you were comparing list of ingredients A with list of ingredients B, chances are you would go with product A.

Let's look at another example. When I used to see the ingredient "flour" declared in a list of ingredients, I would assume it was simply ground up wheat, now I know differently. Flour is one of the most unassuming ingredients in foods today, and one of my favourites to expose!

Not only can flour be labelled six different ways on food labels, it can also contain many additives that are almost never included within the list of ingredients due to the component ingredient exemption in the regulations. For example, flour is allowed to contain a handful of bleaching agents (such as benzoyl peroxide and chlorine[2]— I don't like swimming in chlorine let alone eating it!), which help to impart the bright white colour versus its natural, less desirable, cream colour. Heaven forbid if our bright white breads and cakes were a "less desirable" natural cream colour.

---

2 Department of Justice Canada. *Food and Drugs Act*. "Food and Drug Regulations," B.13.001. [S].

The next time you are in the grocery store, check out an actual package of flour, which has to list all of the ingredients it contains. You may be surprised to find a list of ingredients similar to this one:

- Ingredients: wheat flour, niacin, benzoyl peroxide, iron, ascorbic acid, thiamine mononitrate, alpha-amylase, riboflavin, folic acid.

 Did you know?

The ingredient names "flour," "white flour," "enriched flour," "enriched white flour," "wheat flour," and "enriched wheat flour" can all be used to describe flour on food labels.* Even though some foods include the word *enriched*, the flour in them is not superior. All flour in Canada must meet the same enrichment requirements.

Look for the word *unbleached* as part of the ingredient name; this confirms that bleaching agents, such as benzoyl peroxide and chlorine, were not used in the production of the flour.

* Department of Justice Canada. *Food and Drugs Act.* "Food and Drug Regulations," B.13.001. [S].

 Caution!

The following cookie list of ingredients does not declare the components of the ingredients flour, butter, baking powder, and salt:

- Ingredients: flour, sugar, butter, liquid whole eggs, baking powder, salt.

If the components were declared, however, it may read as –

- Ingredients: flour (wheat flour, niacin, benzoyl peroxide, iron, ascorbic acid, thiamine mononitrate, alpha-amylase, riboflavin, folic acid), butter (cream, salt, colour), liquid whole eggs, baking powder (corn starch, monocalcium phosphate, sodium bicarbonate), salt (calcium silicate, potassium iodide, sodium thiosulphate).

The following are the ingredients, listed in alphabetical order, that the Food and Drug Regulations state as optional for food companies to declare the component ingredients of when added to prepackaged foods. Some ingredients may have their component ingredients hidden no matter what their weight or volume is, whereas others may hide their components only if they are less than a certain percentage of the prepackaged product.

Note that just because an ingredient's components are declared does not necessarily mean that the threshold (percentage in the product) was surpassed, as food companies are free to declare component ingredients at any time.

Ingredients That May Contain
Hidden Component Ingredients in Prepackaged Foods

Ingredient*	When Component Ingredients Can Be Hidden in Prepackaged Products*
Alcoholic beverages	anytime
Alimentary paste	does not contain egg in any form or any flour other than wheat flour
Bacterial culture	anytime
Baking powder	anytime
Breads	anytime
Butter	anytime
Carbonated water	anytime
Cheese	if the total amount of cheese is less than 10% of the product
Chewing gum base	anytime
Chlorinated water	anytime
Cocoa	anytime
Concentrated whey	anytime
Diglycerides	anytime
Flour	anytime
Fluorinated water	anytime
Gelatin	anytime
Graham flour	anytime
Horseradish, olives, pickles, and relish	if the total amount of these ingredients is less than 10% of the product
Hydrolysed plant protein	anytime
Jams, marmalades, and jellies	if the total amount of these ingredients is less than 5% of the product
Lard	anytime

Ingredient*	When Component Ingredients Can Be Hidden in Prepackaged Products*
Leaf lard	anytime
Low-fat cocoa	anytime
Margarine	anytime
Milk	anytime
Modified starches	anytime
Monoglycerides	anytime
Mould culture	anytime
One or more vegetable or animal fats or oils, including hydrogenated, modified, or interesterified oils or fats	if the total amount of these ingredients is less than 15% of the product
Prepared or preserved meat, fish, poultry meat, meat by-product, and poultry meat by-product	if the total amount of these ingredients is less than 10% of the product
Rice	anytime
Salt	anytime
Shortening	anytime
Soy flour	anytime
Starches	anytime
Sweetening agents	anytime
Toasted wheat crumbs	When used in or as a binder, filler, or breading in or on a food product
Vinegars	anytime
Whey	anytime
Whey butter	anytime
Whey butter oil	anytime
Whey powder	anytime
Whole wheat flour	anytime

---

* Department of Justice Canada. *Food and Drugs Act.* "Food and Drug Regulations," B.01.009(1).

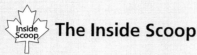 **The Inside Scoop**

Visit the "Inside Scoop" page at www.grainfosalt.ca and type in the password KNOWLEDGE to gain access. Under the "Ingredients" section, look for the complete list with full details of all requirements as per the *Food and Drugs Act,* "Food and Drug Regulations," B.01.009(1).

Empower Yourself!

1. Be aware of the ingredients in the table "Ingredients That May Contain Hidden Component Ingredients in Prepackaged Foods" that are exempt from component declarations and recognize that foods that contain these ingredients may contain hidden component ingredients. If you believe an ingredient should be made up of multiple ingredients, more than likely it should.

2. Try contacting the food company for more information on the component ingredients that have not been declared on the label. Some companies will disclose this information.

3. If you are not able to determine which ingredients are hidden and you are concerned about the product, leave it on the shelf and look for another product that discloses the information you need to feel comfortable.

Caution!

Here's one more for fun! If a frozen pizza contained the following ingredients, it may declare the ingredients as –

- Ingredients: Crust: enriched wheat flour, water, margarine, salt, white vinegar, baking powder. Toppings: mozzarella cheese, pizza sauce (tomatoes, olive oil, salt, sugar, spices), bacon, green olives, seasoned chicken, onions.

... when in fact, if all components were declared, it may read as –

- Ingredients: Crust: enriched wheat flour (wheat flour, niacin, benzoyl peroxide, iron, ascorbic acid, thiamine mononitrate, alpha-amylase, riboflavin, folic acid), water, margarine (canola oil, water, modified palm oil, salt, whey powder, soy lecithin, potassium sorbate, vegetable monoglycerides, citric acid, alpha-tocopherol acetate, calcium disodium EDTA, natural and artificial flavour, carotene, vitamin A palmitate, vitamin D3), salt (calcium silicate, potassium iodide, sodium thiosulphate), white vinegar, baking powder (corn starch, monocalcium phosphate, sodium bicarbonate). Toppings: mozzarella cheese (pasteurized milk, salt [calcium silicate, potassium iodide, sodium thiosulphate], calcium chloride, bacterial culture [lactobacillus], microbial enzyme [*Aspergillus oryzae* RET-1 (pBoel777), *Endothia parasitica*]), pizza sauce (tomatoes, olive oil, salt [calcium silicate, potassium iodide, sodium thiosulphate], sugar, spices), bacon (pork, water, salt, sodium phosphate, sodium erythorbate, sodium nitrite, smoke), green olives (olives, water, salt, lactic acid, potassium sorbate, citric acid), seasoned chicken (chicken, water, salt, sodium phosphate), onions.

CHAPTER 9

Ingredients of Potential Concern

THE FOLLOWING IS "MY TOP FIVE Ingredients-of-Concern List." It is important to be able to recognize these ingredients on food labels and, more importantly, to be able to make educated decisions as to whether you want to put foods that contain these ingredients into your cart and, ultimately, your body.

1. **Synthetic Trans Fats**

   When vegetable oils or fats are described as "hydrogenated" or "partially hydrogenated," it always indicates that a food contains at least some trans fats (the ingredients "shortening" and "margarine" may also indicate that trans fats are present). The ingredient description "partially hydrogenated" is not permitted to appear on food labels in Canada because it may mislead the consumer into thinking that the ingredient does not contain as much trans fat as a fully hydro-genated fat or oil; however, you may still find this ingredient listed on many food labels, as it is permitted on labels in the United States, and some US products are imported into Canada that are not labelled correctly.

The World Health Organization (WHO) has recommended that the total amount of trans fats consumed per day should be less than 1 per cent of your daily energy intake, and Canada's Trans Fat Task Force was formed to develop recommendations and strategies for reducing trans fats in Canadian foods to the lowest level possible.[1]

 Did you know?

Although you may wish to avoid synthetic trans fats, you may also want to consider the amount of naturally occurring trans fat typically found at low levels in some animal-based foods such as dairy prod-ucts, beef, and lamb.

Always check the nutrition facts table for the actual amount of trans fat contained in a specific product per the serving size stated. Remember to compare the serving size back to the net weight to figure out how many servings of the product you are going to consume, and multiply the amounts accordingly.

---

1 Health Canada. "General Questions and Answers on Trans Fat." February 2, 2009, www.hc-sc.gc.ca/fn-an/nutrition/gras-trans-fats/tfa-age_question-eng.php.

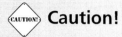 **Caution!**

Food companies are permitted to display the claim "Trans Fat–Free" as long as a food contains less than 0.2 grams of trans fat per serving.* If the food displays this claim and it contains any hydrogenated ingredients, there is a strong possibility that the trans fat amount per serving is closer to 0.2 grams than 0 grams. If you are consuming two, three, or four times the serving size stated, you may end up consuming more trans fat than you desire.

* Regulation for use of the claim "Trans Fat–Free": The food contains less than 0.2 grams of trans fat per reference amount and per serving size stated on the nutrition facts table, as well as 2 grams or less of saturated fat and trans fat combined per serving. The food must also provide 15 per cent or less energy from the sum of saturated fat and trans fat. Department of Justice Canada. *Food and Drugs Act.* "Food and Drug Regulations," Table following B.01.513(22).

2. Sweetening Ingredients

Sweetening ingredients most commonly include sugars, sugar alcohols, and artificial sweeteners. There are multiple ingredients that comprise each of these categories, and it is a good idea to know how to identify them if you are trying to monitor the amount of sugar in your diet. The amount of total sugars must always be declared in the nutrition facts table; however, the following list provides some insight into how to spot the sweetening ingredients within the list of ingredients.

a. Look out for these twenty-five common ingredient names that, in essence, can all mean sugar, keeping in mind that this list is not all-inclusive:

Twenty-Five Common Ingredient Names for Sugar

1. brown sugar, yellow sugar, golden sugar	13. honey
2. cane sugar	14. icing sugar
3. dextrose	15. invert sugar
4. dried glucose syrup	16. lactose
5. evaporated cane juice	17. liquid sugar
6. fructose	18. maltose
7. fructose syrup	19. maple syrup
8. galactose	20. molasses
9. glucose	21. refined sugar syrup
10. glucose-fructose	22. rice, malt, or corn syrup
11. glucose solids	23. sugar
12. glucose syrup	24. sugar/glucose-fructose
	25. sucrose

✓ Quick Tip: If an ingredient name ends in OSE or the word SYRUP, more than likely it is some type of sugar.

b. Look out for these sugar alcohol names:

Ten Common Ingredient Names for Sugar Alcohols

1. erythritol	6. maltitol syrup
2. hydrogenated starch hydrolysates	7. mannitol
	8. sorbitol
3. isomalt	9. sorbitol syrup
4. lactitol	10. xylitol
5. maltitol	

 Caution!

Consuming high quantities of sugar alcohols in foods has been shown to have a laxative effect. In the United States, products that contain sorbitol in an amount that may result in a daily ingestion of 50 grams must display the following statement on their labels: "Excess consumption may have a laxative effect."* Although this statement is not mandatory in Canada, you may still find it on food labels. If you don't see this statement and you notice that a product contains sugar alcohols, remember to check the amount of sugar alcohols indicated on the nutrition facts table. The amount of sugar alcohols found in the product must be expressed in grams; therefore, if you compare the number of grams with the serving size and adjust the amount based on how much of the food you are going to consume, the closer you are to 50 grams the more aware you should be of a potential laxative effect.

* US Federal Department of Agriculture. *Code of Federal Regulations,* Title 21, Section 184.1835(e).

✓ Quick Tip: It is common to find sugar alcohols in products that display the claim "No Sugar Added."

    c. Look out for these artificial sweetener names:

Four Common Ingredient Names for Artificial Sweeteners

1. acesulfame-potassium	3. neotame
2. aspartame	4. sucralose

The Inside Scoop

Visit the "Inside Scoop" page at www.grainofsalt.ca and type in the password KNOWLEDGE to gain access. Refer to the "Ingredients" section for all artificial sweetener requirements as per Division 16, Table IX of the *Food and Drugs Act*, "Food and Drug Regulations."

✓ QuickTip: If you are concerned about aspartame (as well as other artificial sweeteners), look for the statement "Contains Aspartame" or "Sweetened with Aspartame" on the front of labels. You may not have noticed these types of statements before, but they must appear on all foods that contain artificial sweeteners.

Note: When a product contains one or more artificial sweeteners, as well as sugar alcohols and conventional sweetening ingredients such as sugar, they must also be included in the statement. For example, a product that contains aspartame, acesulfame-potassium, sorbitol, and invert sugar would have to display the statement "Contains Aspartame, Acesulfame-Potassium, Sorbitol, and Invert Sugar" or "Sweetened with

Aspartame, Acesulfame-Potassium, Sorbitol, and Invert Sugar" on the front of its label.

 Did you know?

Although maximum levels are controlled and regulated for how much artifical sweetener (as well as all other food additives) can be added to foods, this does not take into consideration a cumulative intake in a given period of time of all foods containing the sweetener.

We are used to seeing aspartame in cola-type beverages, chewing gum, and yogurt, but look out for aspartame that you may also find in the following foods:

- Breakfast cereals
- Beverages, beverage concentrates, beverage mixes*
- Desserts, dessert mixes, toppings, topping mixes, fillings, filling mixes*
- Fruit spreads, purées, and sauces*
- Table syrups
- Salad dressings*
- Peanut and other nut spreads*
- Condiments*
- Confectionary glazes for snack foods
- Sweetened seasoning or coating mixes for snack foods
- Confections and their coatings*

* Products with specific standards of identity within these categories may not allow for aspartame to be added as per Department of Justice Canada's *Food and Drugs Act*, "Food and Drug Regulations," B.16.100, Table IX.

3. Preservatives

The following is a list of twenty-five of the most common preservatives I have seen declared on labels I have reviewed for foods in Canada. (Keep in mind that this list is not all-inclusive.) I try to avoid foods that contain preservatives, and if you are trying to avoid them as well, this list may come in handy.

Twenty-Five Common Ingredient Names
for Preservatives

1. ascorbyl stearate	13. sodium ascorbate
2. butylated hydro xyanisole (BHA)	14 sodium benzoate
	15. sodium bisulphate
3. butylated hydroxytoluene (BHT)	16. sodium diacetate
	17. sodium erythorbate
4. calcium propionate	18. sodium metabisulphite
5. calcium sorbate	19. sodium nitrite and sodium nitrate
6. erythorbic acid	
7. potassium benzoate	20. sodium propionate
8. potassium bisulphite	21. sodium sulphite
9. potassium metabisulphite	22. sorbic acid
10. potassium nitrite and potassium nitrate	23. sulphurous acid
	24. tartaric acid
11. potassium sorbate	25. tertiary butyl hydro-quinone (TBHQ)
12. propionic acid	

Did you know?

In the United States, all chemical preservatives must be declared, along with a description of their function. Statements such as "preservative," "to retard spoilage," "a mould inhibitor," "to help protect flavour," or "to promote colour retention" must appear in the list of ingredients along with the chemical preservative name.* As an example, you may see "sodium benzoate (preservative)" in the list of ingredients.

This additional information helps consumers identify potentially harmful chemical preservatives on their labels. Is it perhaps time we request the same labelling requirements in Canada?

* US Federal Department of Agriculture. *Code of Federal Regulations,* Title 21, Section 101.22(j).

4. Flavour Enhancers

Flavour enhancers are not considered additives in Canada; therefore, the maximum amounts in which they are added to foods are not regulated by the government. If you are concerned about flavour enhancers, look out for these common ingredients (keep in mind that this list is not all-inclusive) that may be enhancing the flavour of your food, but not necessarily the healthfulness.

Six Common Ingredient Names for Flavour Enhancers

1. calcium inosinate	4. hydrolysed plant proteins
2. disodium guanylate	5. monosodium glutamate (MSG)
3. ethyl maltol	6. sodium ribonucleotides

☑ Quick Tip: Salt is one of the most common flavour enhancers added to processed foods. Always remember to check the amount of sodium and the corresponding per cent daily value indicated on the nutrition facts table per serving size stated. Remember to adjust these numbers based on how much of the food you are planning to consume and if your calorie requirements are less than or more than 2,000 calories a day. If you are not sure how much sodium you should be consuming, talk to your health-care provider.

5. Artificial Colours

The following ten artificial colours are permitted in food in Canada;[2] however, it may be difficult to determine if these colours are added to foods because the class name "colour" is permitted to be used when multiple different colours have been added to a product.

2 Department of Justice Canada. *Food and Drugs Act.* "Food and Drug Regulations," Division 16, Table III.

Ten Common Ingredient Names for Artificial Colours

1. allura red	6. fast green FCF
2. amaranth	7. indigotine
3. brilliant blue FCF	8. ponceau SX
4. citrus red no. 2	9. tartrazine
5. erythrosine	10. sunset yellow FCF

 Quick Tip: When only natural colours are added to processed foods, food companies like to display the claim "No Artificial Colours" on their labels. Look for this claim; otherwise, my rule of thumb is to protect yourself by assuming that artificial colours have been added.

? Did you know?

When artificial colours are added to foods in Europe, the following warning statement must appear on the label: "May Have an Adverse Effect on Activity and Attention in Children."* Although we may never see a claim such as this one on food labels in Canada, at the very least I'm sure you would agree that artificial colours should be labelled using the ingredient name "artificial colour" instead of "colour."

* Regulation (EC) No. 1333/2008 of the European Parliament and of the Council of 16 December 2008 on Food Additives, Annex V.

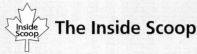

The Inside Scoop

There are some restricted uses for artificial colours in food products sold in Canada. Visit the "Inside Scoop" page at www.grainofsalt.ca and type in the password KNOWLEDGE to gain access. Refer to the "Ingredients" section for more information on which foods can contain which colours as per Division 16, Table III of the *Food and Drugs Act*, "Food and Drug Regulations."

Empower Yourself!

1. Use the information in this chapter while shopping to make more informed purchasing decisions. These are the top five groups of ingredients I try to avoid, but you may have more. Don't compromise the healthfulness of your foods based on sale prices or promotions; stick to your beliefs and leave the products that contain ingredients you wish to avoid on the shelf!

2. There are a variety of books and smart-phone apps (key word: food additives) that provide a quick reference to help you navigate the complex world of chemical food additives and preservatives. Although these resources are often based on US regulations, you will typically find information about many of the food additives found in foods sold in Canada. Look up the potential health effects of the ingredients found in foods you are considering purchasing and decide if you should put that food in your cart or leave it on the shelf.

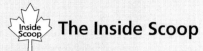 **The Inside Scoop**

Still feeling overwhelmed? Consider buying organic! Organic foods are permitted to contain only a small amount of non-organic ingredients, of which none are permitted to be synthetic (with exceptions).* Visit the "Inside Scoop" page at www.grainofsalt.ca and type in the password KNOWLEDGE to gain access. Under the "All Things Organic" section, look for more information on non-organic ingredients permitted in organic products.

* Canadian General Standards Board. *Organic Production Systems General Principles and Management Standards* 1.4, "Prohibited Substances, Methods or Ingredients in Organic Production and Handling." CAN/CGSB-32.310-2006, amended October 2008, and *Organic Products Systems Permitted Substances Lists,* CAN/CGSB-32.311-2006, amended August 2011.

CHAPTER 10

Highlighted Ingredient Claims

I CAN IMAGINE YOUR SURPRISE WHEN YOU bring home chocolate chip cookies only to realize that the chocolate chips do not contain real chocolate, or crab cakes that are made with imitation crab instead of real crabmeat, or how about strawberry cereal bars that do not contain real strawberries, but instead contain only strawberry flavour and colour? Unfortunately, quality, wholesome, real ingredients are highlighted in product names, descriptions, and images on prepackaged processed food labels that do not actually contain these ingredients, and many consumers are none the wiser, unless they read the list of ingredients.

Technically, when an ingredient is highlighted on the front panel of a label, it should be accompanied by a statement regarding the amount of the ingredient that is actually present in the food.[1] For example, if a cereal bar that contained 5 per cent strawberries highlighted the word *strawberry* in the product name, it should display a statement such as "Contains 5% Strawberries" under the product name. Unfortunately, statements such as these are rarely found on food labels.

---

1 Canadian Food Inspection Agency. *Guide to Food Labelling and Advertising*, Section 4.2.3.

The Grey Areas: How Food Companies Bend the Rules

A few years ago, rather confusing guidance was given by the CFIA to food companies on how to properly display highlighted ingredient claims. Because the information was *only* guidance and not regulation (law), very little of it was actually implemented. The highlighted ingredient-claims guidance included a breakdown of how to label the following four categories:

1. Imitation ingredients
2. Flavour ingredients
3. Essential ingredients
4. Premium ingredients

The concept of imitation ingredients seems simple enough. If a food contains an ingredient that is an imitation of a real ingredient (e.g., crab versus imitation crab), and that ingredient is highlighted, the food company should include the word *imitation* as part of the claim (e.g., "Contains Imitation Crabmeat"). For obvious reasons, food companies try to avoid placing the word imitation on their labels as it relates to the food, and, typically, fanciful names (e.g., "Surimi Crab" versus "Imitation Crab") are used instead.

The concept of flavour ingredients is also fairly well understood (but not necessarily implemented). If the ingredient that is part of a highlighted ingredient claim comprises less than 2 per cent of the product, or is a natural or artificial flavour, the word *flavour* has to be added to the ingredient name that is highlighted in the product name or claim. For example, strawberry cereal bars that contain 1 per cent real strawberries, as well as strawberry cereal bars that simply contain strawberry flavour, should be labelled "Strawberry-Flavoured Cereal Bars." Technically, cereal bars with over 2 per cent strawberries could be called "Strawberry Cereal Bars," but they should have a statement indicating the percentage of strawberries found in the product, as noted previously.

When the CFIA's guidance on highlighted ingredient claims was first released, there was a lot of confusion within the food industry. Even as a food label specialist, this was the first time that I had heard the terms *essential ingredients* and *premium ingredients* being used in the context of their use in highlighted ingredient claims. The basic principle was that if an ingredient is being highlighted, ingredients that are similar should also be highlighted if that ingredient isn't present in the product in a substantially higher amount. For example, a bran flake cereal that contains 20 per cent bran flakes, and also contains 18 per cent corn flakes and 18 per cent rice flakes, should not be permitted to be labelled "Bran Flake Cereal." An acceptable name would be "Bran, Corn, and Rice Flake Cereal," or "20% Bran Flake Cereal."

This concept seemed fair, but if only partially implemented, the guidance presented the risk of hampering the competitiveness of certain products if some food companies declared the similar ingredients, while others did not.

Juices are a common culprit of selective highlighting of only certain premium ingredients. There are currently a great number of juices on the market that highlight premium fruit juices such as mango, blood orange, kiwi, strawberry, or blueberry, but which are composed mostly of apple and/or grape juices.

In general, food companies are not quick to declare percentages of highlighted ingredients on their labels because most of the time the percentages are much lower than consumers assume them to be. Would you buy a crab cake that was called "5% Crab Cake"? They also may not be willing to highlight imitation or less expensive similar ingredients on their labels when competitive products on the market are not doing so.

 Caution!

If you find a label that highlights an ingredient, and that ingredient falls under an exemption of component ingredients (please see chapter 8 for a list of ingredients that do not have to declare components when found in prepackaged products), check to see if the component ingredients have been declared.

Consider this example: A pizza product highlights the topping bacon on the front of a label. When you read the list of ingredients, you see that only bacon is declared, but not its component ingredients, such as pork, water, salt, sodium phosphate, sodium erythorbate, sodium nitrite, and smoke, which are typically found in bacon. As mentioned in chapter 8, prepared or preserved meats (which include bacon) do not have to declare components when their total amount is less than 10 per cent of a prepackaged product. Therefore, because component ingredients were not declared, you instantly know that the product contains less than 10 per cent bacon, which doesn't seem like much when the word bacon is highlighted across the front of the package.

Let's look at an example. I was out shopping one day looking for a dip to serve at a party, and I found one that was called "Artichoke and Asiago Dip." Naturally, I assumed that both artichokes and Asiago cheese would be listed within the first few ingredients. Instead, I was shocked to find that the dip did not contain artichoke pieces at all, but instead contained artichoke water, and more cream cheese than Asiago cheese. In my opinion, a more appropriate name for this product might have been "Artichoke Water and Cream Cheese Dip with Asiago Cheese"—not quite as appealing. If I hadn't read the list of ingredients and compared it with the name of the product, I would have been very disappointed when I served what I thought was a fancy premium dip that was actually only average at best.

Let's consider another example. I recently went shopping for cereal and found a label that highlighted pomegranates on the front of the package. The word *pomegranate* was displayed in a bold, prominent font, along with appealing images of fresh pomegranates. Under these images in a much smaller font was the text "Natural Pomegranate Flavour." When I read the list of ingredients, however, it was clear that this product did not contain pomegranate pieces at all, but instead contained dried cranberries that I assume were coated with and/or infused with sugar, pomegranate juice, glycerol, and vegetable oil.

Furthermore, this food company pushed the limits even further by spacing the ingredients out within the list of ingredients so that the only ingredient that had substantial white space on either side of it was the pomegranate juice concentrate; however, the substantial white space was found only before and after the word *pomegranate*. At a glance, the one word you would see within the list of ingredients was pomegranate, which means you may miss that it was actually pomegranate juice concentrate and was only a *component* ingredient of the dried cranberries. They also displayed romance text indicating that pomegranates are packed with vitamins and minerals and are known for their antioxidant content. It may be true that pomegranates offer some specific benefits; however, in relation to this product, I would consider the information misleading as I don't believe there could be more than a couple of drops of pomegranate juice concentrate in or on each of the tiny dried cranberries found in the package.

How about another cereal example just for fun! Honey and almond granola cereals are popular in the cereal aisle, but have you ever read the list of ingredients to see where the ingredients honey and almonds are listed? I once came across a label that displayed the following list of ingredients:

Honey and Almond Granola

- Ingredients: rolled oats, brown sugar, wheat flakes, crisp rice, modified milk ingredients, oat bran, soybean oil, sliced almonds, apple juice concentrate, honey, soy lecithin, natural flavour.

Highlighting the almonds on the front of the label seems appropriate, as the product did contain sliced almonds and no similar ingredients (such as other nuts); however, honey is the third ingredient from the end of the list of ingredients (which means it is contained in the product in the third-least amount), and other similar ingredients appear much more prominently in the list of ingredients. Brown sugar and apple juice concentrate were each listed ahead of honey (by weight), and thus most likely contributed more of the sweetness than the honey. Therefore, instead of the description "Honey and Almond Granola," a more appropriate description may have been "Brown Sugar, Apple Juice Concentrate, Honey, and Almond Granola."

☑ Quick Tip: Remember that ingredients are declared in descending order by weight. This particular honey and almond granola declared the ingredient "soybean oil" before the ingredient "sliced almonds"; if you missed this, would you be upset? Try not to focus on only one aspect of the list of ingredients. Ingredient-list reading is most efficient when each of the following five points are considered:

1. The order of ingredients.
2. The number of similar ingredients that may be present (i.e., how many different sweetening ingredients does the product contain?).
3. The healthfulness of the ingredients (based on your own personal criteria).
4. The types and number of additives present.
5. Natural ingredients versus synthetic ingredients.

Empower Yourself!

1. If you see a label that highlights a premium ingredient, remember to always check the list of ingredients to make sure similar less desirable ingredients are not declared before it, indicating that they are present in a greater amount.
2. Look for words such as *dried, flavour, artificial,* and *imitation* in the list of ingredients. These words may indicate that the highlighted ingredient is not present in the product in the form or suggested prevalence that was highlighted.

3. Look for a declaration of the percentage of the ingredient that is highlighted on the front of the package (e.g., "20% Bran Flake Cereal"). If you don't see a percentage, my rule of thumb is to always assume the highlighted ingredient is present in the product in an amount that is lower than you may think it should be.

4. Use caution when ingredients that may typically contribute positive or negative effects to health are highlighted, such as foods high in vitamins or minerals that you may wish to include in your diet, or conversely, foods high in sodium, sugars, or fats that you may wish to avoid. If you aren't comfortable with the information provided on the label, look for another product that discloses the information you need to feel comfortable.

CHAPTER 11

Nutrition Facts Tables

WHEN STANDARDIZED NUTRITION LABELLING became fully mandatory in Canada in 2007, food companies were very confused with the new regulations. Up until this point, companies were able to place just about any type of nutritional information on labels that they saw fit. As long as the information was truthful, they could, in essence, display the nutrition information for the nutrients they chose, and in any sort of table format.

The new standardized nutrition labelling regulations introduced a mandatory consistent table format for all labels, mandatory nutrients that have to be displayed within the table, and mandatory rules (called *rounding rules*) for determining the values that are displayed. In an effort to help food companies better understand the new requirements, the CFIA released their almost 350-page nutrition labelling toolkit for companies to review, which begs the question, if the CFIA and food companies need a 350-page toolkit to teach them how to create nutrition facts tables, how are consumers expected to be able to easily read and understand the information at a glance while grocery shopping?

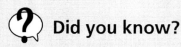 Did you know?

Although most labels display what is known as a *consistent vertical bilingual standard nutrition facts table* (please see the image on page 97), food companies can display different table formats and sizes, and they have options to display bilingual tables or one English table and one French table.

You may find what is called a *simplified table* on some labels that declares only the calorie value and the amounts of fat, carbohydrate, and protein because the amounts of the other core nutrients are zero; you may find tables that include information for multiple products or for the product when it is prepared with additional ingredients; and you may even find some tables that list the information horizontally rather than in the conventional vertical format.

 The Inside Scoop

Visit the "Inside Scoop" page at www.grainofsalt.ca and type in the password KNOWLEDGE to gain access. Refer to the "Nutrition Facts Table" section and look for the heading "Different Nutrition Facts Table Formats" to better familiarize yourself with the different nutrition facts table formats that may be displayed on food labels in Canada.

Reading and understanding the nutrition facts table is definitely one of the essential steps to empowering yourself with the information you need to make more healthful choices when purchasing prepackaged processed food products. The following are the three main sections that you should review each time you read a nutrition facts table:

- Section 1: Serving size
- Section 2: Amount of each nutrient declared (or the nutrients you are interested in or concerned about)
- Section 3: Per cent daily value for each nutrient (or the nutrients you are interested in or concerned about)

Let's take a closer look at the three sections.

Section 1: Serving Size

Nutrition Facts
Valeur nutritive

Per 1 can (350 mL)
pour 1 canette (350 mL)

Amount / Teneur	% Daily Value / % valeur quotidienne
Calories / Calories 130	
Fat / Lipides 1.5 g	2 %
Saturated / saturés 1 g + Trans / trans 0 g	5 %
Cholesterol / Cholestérol 0 mg	
Sodium / Sodium 55 mg	2 %
Carbohydrate / Glucides 29 g	10 %
Fibre / Fibres 0 g	0 %
Sugars / Sucres 26 g	
Protein / Protéines 0 g	
Vitamin A / Vitamine A	0 %
Vitamin C / Vitamine C	20 %
Calcium / Calcium	4 %
Iron / Fer	2 %

Serving Size

The only way to put the information on the nutrition facts table in context is to understand the serving size that is stated. The CFIA has provided food companies with recommended ranges for serving sizes for each of the major product categories (e.g., a serving size range of 30 to 40 grams is recommended for cookies, and a serving size range of 60 to 250 millilitres is recommended for ice cream);[1] however, these recommendations are often broad ranges and not one specific amount, and that is why you may find a great variance in the serving sizes declared on similar products in the market.

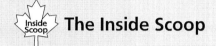 **The Inside Scoop**

Visit the "Inside Scoop" page at www.grainofsalt.ca and type in the password KNOWLEDGE to gain access. Refer to the "Nutrition Facts Table" section and look for a full list of recommended serving sizes for foods in Canada.

Serving sizes should always be stated as a familiar household measure, for example, 1 tbsp, 1 cup, or 2 pieces, and as a corresponding weight or volume, for example, 15 mL, 250 mL, or 100 g. A typical serving size may read –
- "Per 1 tbsp (15 mL),"
- "Per 1 cup (250 mL)," or
- "Per 2 pieces (100 g)."

---

1 Canadian Food Inspection Agency. *Guide to Food Labelling and Advertising*, Section 6.2, Table 6-3(8)(53).

Seems simple enough, but serving sizes can create confusion when you are comparing products. The weight of "a piece" may not be the same for each of the two competing products you are comparing. The weight of one cookie may be 20 grams and another may be 30 grams. In this case, it would be necessary to multiply all of the numbers seen on the nutrition facts table of the first cookie by 1.5 in order to accurately compare the two products.

Serving sizes can also become confusing when you eat more than one serving of a product. Nutrient information based on a serving size of one cookie will no longer be applicable if you eat two, three, or more cookies. It is so important to remember to multiply the nutrient and per cent daily value information by the number of servings you have consumed for accurate information.

Finally, make sure you check the serving size in relation to the net quantity to gain a clear understanding of the amount of each nutrient you are about to consume. If a can of soup indicates a per cent daily value for sodium of 50 per cent per 250 mL serving, but the can contains 500 mL (two times the serving size), and you intend on eating the full can, you will have to make sure the nutrient amounts and per cent daily values are altered. In this case, the per cent daily value for sodium would increase from 50 per cent to 100 per cent (2 × 50 per cent) if you ate the full can (which is typical), and it may be outside of your target range.

Did you know?

Servings per container information on nutrition facts tables saves you the work of having to compare the serving size displayed with the net quantity to gain an understanding of how many servings you may consume if you consumed the entire contents of the package.

If the servings per container information was displayed on the nutrition facts table in the soup example on page 99, the serving size declaration would read –

- "Per 1 cup (250 mL)"
- "Servings Per Container 2"

In this case, you would instantly know that you would need to multiply every nutrient amount and per cent daily value by two if you intended on eating the entire can of soup.

In the United States, it is mandatory to display the number of servings per container on the nutrition facts table directly under the serving-size declaration; however, in Canada this requirement is optional, and I have yet to review or see a nutrition facts table that displays this information. Perhaps it is time to request that Health Canada make this requirement mandatory!

Section 2: Amount of Each Nutrient

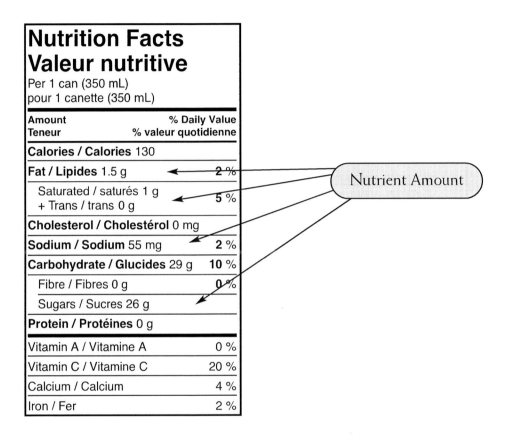

Every nutrition facts table must declare the calorie value of the food plus information for thirteen core nutrients, as seen on the nutrition facts table example above. The amount of each nutrient (excluding vitamins and minerals, which are declared only as per cent daily values), is declared in grams or milligrams in the nutrition facts table, perhaps making it easier for consumers to visualize the amounts. Consumers are typically looking for lower calorie, fat, saturated fat, trans fat, cholesterol, sodium, and sugars values, and higher fibre, vitamin, and mineral values.

 Did you know?

Some nutrition facts tables may display additional nutrients such as potassium, folic acid, niacin, and riboflavin. The thirteen core nutrients displayed on nutrition facts tables are considered important to the health of Canadians; however, many foods contain additional nutrients, and just because they are not displayed does not necessarily mean they are not in the food.

 Did you know?

Not all food products in Canada must display a nutrition facts table. The following foods are exempt from displaying a table:*
- Foods that may express the calorie value and all nutrient values as zero, such as some spices and bottled waters.
- Beverages with an alcohol content of more than 0.5 per cent.
- Fresh fruits and vegetables without added ingredients (includes oranges with colour and fruits and vegetables coated with paraffin wax or petrolatum); fresh herbs (but not dried herbs); sprouts; mixtures of fruits and vegetables, such as bagged mixed salads (without dressing, croutons, etc.); and fruits and vegetables that are minimally processed (e.g., washed, peeled, cut up, and shredded).

- Raw, single-ingredient meat, meat by-product, poultry meat, and poultry meat by-product. This does not include prepackaged ground meat, ground meat by-product, ground poultry meat, and ground poultry meat by-product that must always carry a nutrition facts table.

- Raw, single-ingredient marine or freshwater animal products (such as fish and crustaceans).

- Foods sold only in the retail establishment where the product is prepared and processed from its ingredients, including products made from a premix when an ingredient other than water is added to the premix. A nutrition facts table is required when only water is added to a premix or when a product is only baked, cooked, etc., on the premises without the addition of other ingredients.

- Foods sold only at a roadside stand, craft show, flea market, fair, farmers' market, and sugar bush by the individual who prepared and processed the product.

- Individual servings of foods that are sold for immediate consumption (e.g., sandwiches or ready-made salads), when these have not been subjected to a process or special packaging, such as modified atmosphere packaging, to extend their durable life.

- Foods sold only in the retail establishment where the product is packaged, if the product is labelled by means of a sticker and has an available display surface of less than 200 cm^2.

- Prepackaged confections, commonly known as one-bite confections, that are sold individually (e.g., small individually wrapped candies and mints).

- Prepackaged individual portions of foods that are solely intended to be served by a restaurant or other commercial enterprise with meals or snacks (such as crackers and creamers).
- A variety of cow's and goat's milk products sold in refillable glass containers.

Although one-bite confections, an individual portion served with meals, and milk in glass containers never lose their exemption, the other items listed above lose their exempt status and are a required to carry a nutrition facts table when [†] –

- A vitamin or mineral is added to the product.
- A vitamin or mineral nutrient is declared as a component of an ingredient (other than flour).
- Aspartame, sucralose, or acesulfame-potassium is added to the product.
- The product is ground meat, ground meat by-product, ground poultry meat, or ground poultry meat by-product.
- The label or advertisement contains one or more of the following:
    - A nutritional reference or nutrient content claim.
    - A biological role claim.
    - A health claim.
    - A health-related name, statement, logo, symbol, seal of approval, or other proprietary mark of a third party.
    - The phrase "Nutrition Facts," "Valeur nutritive," or "Valeurs nutritives."

* Department of Justice Canada. *Food and Drugs Act.* "Food and Drug Regulations," B.01.401(2) and B.01.401(3).

† Ibid.

A quick review of the nutrient amounts is helpful when you are looking for specific nutrient values to be as close to zero as possible. For example, I always check the trans fat value on nutrition facts tables and personally only buy foods that declare an amount of 0 grams (or as close to 0 grams as possible).

For the nutrients that you have not set target intake levels for, the specific amounts may not always be so helpful. For example, ideally, how many grams of carbohydrates should you eat in one serving? Is 10 grams okay, or is 20 grams okay?

If you have received specific instructions from your health-care provider on the amount of a nutrient you should consume in a day, the nutrient amounts may be useful; however, when I am looking at or comparing nutrition facts tables, I prefer to use the per cent daily value information to put my nutrient intakes into perspective.

Nutrition Facts
Valeur nutritive

Per 1 can (350 mL)
pour 1 canette (350 mL)

Amount Teneur	% Daily Value % valeur quotidienne
Calories / Calories 130	
Fat / Lipides 1.5 g	2 %
Saturated / saturés 1 g + Trans / trans 0 g	5 %
Cholesterol / Cholestérol 0 mg	
Sodium / Sodium 55 mg	2 %
Carbohydrate / Glucides 29 g	10 %
Fibre / Fibres 0 g	0 %
Sugars / Sucres 26 g	
Protein / Protéines 0 g	
Vitamin A / Vitamine A	0 %
Vitamin C / Vitamine C	20 %
Calcium / Calcium	4 %
Iron / Fer	2 %

Section 3: Per Cent Daily Value

% Daily Value

The per cent daily value (or "% DV") can be used, in theory, to quickly gauge how healthful or unhealthful a food is within the context of the recommendations made by Health Canada. The per cent daily value is calculated based on the amount of a specific nutrient in a product divided by —

1. the *recommended daily intake* amounts for vitamins and minerals, or
2. the *reference standards* for nutrients other than vitamins and minerals (i.e., fat, saturated plus trans fat, cholesterol, sodium, potassium [if it is declared], total carbohydrate, and fibre).

✓ Quick Tip: **If you are looking for foods rich in specific nutrients, look for higher percentages, and if you do not want to consume too much of certain nutrients, look for lower percentages. Health Canada's interactive "The % Daily Value" webpage provides the following rule of thumb: "5% DV or less is a little and 15% DV or more is a lot for all nutrients."[2]**

The Recommended Daily Intakes (RDI) for the four core vitamins and minerals for average Canadians (over two years old) based on a 2,000-calorie diet are[3] —

- Vitamin A: 1,000 RE (retinol equivalent)
- Vitamin C: 60 mg
- Calcium: 1,100 mg
- Iron: 14 mg

---

2 Health Canada. "The % Daily Value." January 19, 2012, www.hc-sc.gc.ca/fn-an/label-etiquet/nutrition/cons/dv-vq/index-eng.php.

3 Canadian Food Inspection Agency. *Guide to Food Labelling and Advertising*, 6.3.2, and Department of Justice Canada. *Food and Drugs Act*. "Food and Drug Regulations," D.01.013 Table 1, and D.02.006 Table 1.

The reference standards for average Canadians (over two years old) based on a 2,000-calorie diet are[4] –

- Fat: 65 g
- Saturated fat plus trans fat: 20 g
- Cholesterol: 300 mg
- Sodium: 2,400 mg
- Potassium: 3,500 mg
- Carbohydrate: 300 g
- Fibre: 25 g

 Caution!

Although the per cent daily value displayed on nutrition facts tables for sodium is based on a reference standard of 2,400 mg, Health Canada confirms on their webpage "Sodium: Questions and Answers" that "the recommended intake for people aged 1 year and older, ranges from 1,000 mg per day to 1,500 mg per day."*

To put this into context, a product that declares 100 per cent of the daily value for sodium per serving should actually declare it as 160 per cent if the per cent daily value was based on the recommended intake of 1,500 mg per day rather than the reference standard of 2,400 mg per day.

* Health Canada. "Sodium: Questions and Answers: What is the recommended intake?" December 29, 2010, www.hc-sc.gc.ca/fn-an/nutrition/sodium/qa-sodium-qr-eng.php#a4.

4 Canadian Food Inspection Agency. *Guide to Food Labelling and Advertising*, 6.3.4, and Department of Justice Canada. *Food and Drugs Act.* "Food and Drug Regulations," Table to B.01.001.1(2).

◇ Caution!

Per cent daily values are calculated based on recommended daily intakes and reference standards that are based on an average adult's consumption of 2,000 calories a day. If your calorie needs are less than or greater than 2,000 calories a day, the per cent daily values displayed on nutrition facts tables will have to be adjusted accordingly. For example, a nutrition facts table that displays a per cent daily value for carbohydrates of 10 per cent means the following:

- If you aim to consume 2,000 calories a day, one serving of this particular food would provide 10 per cent* of the total amount of carbohydrates consumed in one day based on the reference standard.

- If you aim to consume 1,500 calories a day, one serving of the same food would provide 13 per cent* of the total amount of carbohydrates consumed that day based on the reference standard.

- If you aim to consume 2,500 calories a day, one serving of the same food would provide 8 per cent* of the total amount of carbohydrates consumed that day based on the reference standard.

Talk to your health-care provider to determine your daily calorie needs, and to gain a better understanding of how to adjust the per cent daily values on the nutrition facts tables of the foods you are buying.

* Per cent Daily Values are based on rounded percentages. Department of Justice Canada. *Food and Drugs Act.* "Food and Drug Regulations," Table following B.01.401(7).

(✓) Quick Tip: If your health-care provider has recommended daily intake goals that are different from Health Canada's recommended daily intakes and reference standards, you will need to adjust these numbers accordingly.

In order to use the per cent daily value information productively, try keeping track of the percentages of the nutrients you are concerned about and adding the percentages together as you continue eating foods throughout the day. When you get to 100 per cent (or another specific percentage recommended by your health-care provider), you have met your daily target (based on a 2,000-calorie diet).

Empower Yourself!

1. Always read the serving size on the nutrition facts table first to gain an understanding of what the serving size means, how it relates to the net quantity, how many servings of the product you are actually going to eat, and how it differs from products you may be comparing it with.

2. Read the nutrient amounts that matter to you. If you are trying to avoid trans fats, look for a trans fat amount as close to zero as possible; if you are trying to increase your fibre, look for a fibre value that meets your dietary requirements.

3. Focus on the per cent daily values. Remember that per cent daily values are calculated based on reference standards and recommended daily intakes for average Canadians (over two years old), and are based on a 2,000-calorie diet. If your calorie needs are different, you will have to adjust the numbers accordingly.

4. Talk to your health-care provider to gain a better understanding of which nutrients you should focus on and how much of each nutrient you should be consuming each day. Just because the nutrition facts table includes per cent daily values does not mean that they are specific to your dietary needs.

CHAPTER 12

How Food Companies Come Up
with the Numbers on Nutrition Facts Tables

HAVE YOU EVER STOPPED AND THOUGHT about where the numbers that are displayed on nutrition facts tables come from? Or if they are accurate and reflective of the food that is in the package? Consumers seem to be genuinely concerned about the validity of nutrition and health-based claims on labels, but what about the actual numbers that are displayed in the tables?

The task of determining a product's nutrition information is left up to the food companies, and we have to hope that they use valid Canadian-recommended methods to determine nutrient amounts, understand Canadian nutrient requirements and rounding rules, use Canadian-recommended serving size ranges, and display the information accurately using a Canadian-required nutrition facts table format.

It can be very challenging when working with international companies whose rules are completely different from Canada's. For example, Canada includes the amount of dietary fibre in a product as part of the total carbohydrate amount, but not every country does. If a product is high in fibre, and the fibre value isn't included in the total carbohydrate amount declared, you could be led to believe the product contains less carbohydrate than it actually does if the value is not calculated based on Canadian requirements.

Like all information displayed on food labels, we are at the mercy of the food companies to display accurate information. We have to trust that companies are being diligent with their nutrition information; however, you must keep in mind that some nutrients make a food much more appealing when they are declared on the low side (e.g., trans fats) and some make a food more appealing when they are declared on the high side (e.g., vitamins and minerals).

The Grey Areas: How Food Companies Bend the Rules

There are two areas that relate to nutrition labelling that have the potential to be exploited by food companies. The first is a 20 per cent tolerance range permitted for nutrient amounts declared, and the second is the method by which food companies come up with the numbers displayed on nutrition facts tables.

Twenty Per Cent Tolerance Range

One of the areas that has potential to be exploited is the CFIA's "Nutrition Compliance Test" that allows for a 20 per cent tolerance range for nutrient amounts.[1] This tolerance range, in theory, protects food companies from small variations in product content, seasonal variations of

---

1 When vitamins and minerals are added to foods as specified in Department of Justice Canada's *Food and Drugs Act*, "Food and Drug Regulations," Table following D.03.002, there is no tolerance range permitted.

ingredients, and variations in sourcing of ingredients. A bright red tomato that is in season may be more nutrient-rich than an out-of-season tomato that is added to a processed food; similar ingredients sourced from different countries may have different nutrient profiles, depending on how they are grown and the climate; or slightly more or less of an ingredient may be added to a product when it is manufactured.

The problem is that some food companies may use this tolerance range to their advantage by manipulating nutrition information on labels. For example, nutrients that consumers like to see lower, such as saturated fat, trans fat, and sodium, may be declared 20 per cent lower than calculated in order to create an impression that the food is more healthful than it may be. A saturated fat value of 10 grams could be declared as low as 8 grams. Rest assured, this doesn't happen often; however, I have seen it happen, and it only further solidifies my advice to read your labels with a grain of salt.

How Food Companies Come Up with the Numbers

The second grey area is the method a food company chooses to calculate the amounts of each of the nutrients declared on the nutrition facts table. There are three main ways that a company can come up with the numbers that are displayed on their labels:

1. They have their products analyzed by accredited laboratories that specialize in nutritional analysis.
2. They calculate the nutrient content using a nutrition database.
3. They copy another similar product's nutrition information.

Laboratory Analysis

The most accurate method, and the method that is recommended by the CFIA for determining the nutrition information of a product, is laboratory analysis.[2] Laboratory analysis is the most accurate method of determining nutrient content because it analyzes the food after it has been processed; therefore, the nutrient values are reflective of the food that is found in the package. In a perfect world, all nutrition facts tables displayed on labels would be reflective of an analysis conducted by an accredited Canadian laboratory.

Not only does the CFIA recommend this method, they also define the specific testing methods that should be used for the analysis of each of the core nutrients shown on the nutrition facts table.[3] Given these recommended tests, all accredited labs, whether in Canada or abroad, should produce consistent and accurate results.

One would think (maybe hope) that all companies would use this method to determine nutrient amounts, but they don't. It is expensive to have products analyzed by labs. Companies with deep pockets typically send their products to labs, but some food companies cannot afford the high price tag or, even worse, don't care to make the investment.

When companies opt out of using a lab to determine nutrition information, the next-best method is to use a nutrition database.

Nutrition Database

Nutrition databases are amazing tools that have been used by product developers, dietitians, and nutritionists for many years. They are large

---

2 Canadian Food Inspection Agency. "Nutrition Labelling Compliance Test," Appendix Laboratory Issues, Methods of Analysis.
3 Ibid.

computer databases that contain nutrition information for virtually every ingredient you can think of. Nutrition information for foods such as lettuce, apples, eggs, and chicken breast; common multi-ingredient foods such as white bread, ketchup, and mayonnaise; and a large variety of other common ingredients, such as salt and spices, that are found in foods can be found in nutrition databases.

Based on my experience, I would estimate that well over half of food companies selling food in Canada use nutrition databases to calculate the values for their nutrition facts tables. Thankfully, there is one widely used nutrition database that helps to create some consistency in nutrition labelling; however, there are also less reputable databases that increase the chances of food labels displaying inaccurate information.

The problem with databases is that the nutrition information is not always fully representative of the ingredients that are contained in a specific product. For example, if a product contains tomato sauce, there is no guarantee that the tomato sauce represented in the database is an exact match in formulation to the tomato sauce used in the actual product. Also, database information does not take the specific processing methods used for foods into consideration. For example, the nutrition information for cooked tomatoes in a database may not be representative of a product that contains cooked tomatoes that is then further processed at high temperatures.

Did you know?

Some vitamins, such as vitamin C, will break down over time. When using laboratory analysis to determine nutrition information, vitamin breakdown can be taken into consideration by having samples of a product analyzed that are closer to the end of their shelf life. For example, if a product has a shelf life of ninety days, it would be ideal to analyze the vitamin C content of the product as close to the ninety-day mark as possible. When using nutrient databases, vitamin breakdown for a specific product being analyzed is not typically taken into consideration, adding yet another potential level of inaccuracy to nutrient values declared on nutrition facts tables.

Copying Nutrition Information

Believe it or not, the nutrition information can become even less trustworthy than information generated from random databases. When it comes to food labels, I have seen it all. Some companies don't want to make an additional investment in their products and simply copy nutrition information from labels of similar products and place it on their own labels. What better way to stay competitive than to match their competition by copying their nutrition facts table word for word. There can be major variations in nutrient values between even the most similar products, and therefore the nutrition information on these labels may not be representative of the actual food in the package.

Unfortunately, we have no way of knowing which method was used on the foods we eat, and the CFIA does not have the resources to verify nutrition information displayed on every food label in Canada. As a general rule of thumb, I am more trusting of nutrition information displayed on labels of products produced by large national companies, and less trusting of information displayed on labels of small manufacturers or importers. Keep in mind, however, that this is a general rule of thumb. The importer I worked for was diligent about labelling their foods accurately, and some of the larger companies I have worked for have not displayed the same level of diligence.

✓ Quick Tip: Check the trademarked name, brand name, or dealer name and address to see if you recognize, and perhaps trust, the company.

Empower Yourself!

1. If nutrient amounts and/or per cent daily values seem unusually high or low, check the list of ingredients for a better understanding of possible errors. For example, if hydrogenated oils are listed in the list of ingredients, but the trans fat value is declared as zero, it is possible that the value may not be accurate.
2. Remember that we are at the mercy of food companies to put accurate information on nutrition facts tables, and for this reason you should always read nutrition facts tables with a grain of salt.

CHAPTER 13

Nutrition Claims

NUTRITION IS TOP OF MIND FOR MANY consumers today, and what better way to market a product than to make claims about its nutritional merit.

Within the context of making nutrition claims, claims regarding nutrient content are fairly well regulated by the government; they must meet specific requirements and must be declared using the exact text that is provided for in the regulations. For example, "Fat-Free" means the food contains less than 0.5 grams of fat per reference amount and per the serving size that is stated on the label.[1]

Nutrient content claims (i.e., "Fat-Free," "Low Cholesterol," "Source of Fibre") are based on a reference amount and the serving size as stated on the label. Reference amounts were created to ensure consistency across labels because serving sizes can vary so drastically for similar products made by different companies.

Consider this example: The reference amount for cookies is 30 grams;[2] therefore, if a fat-free claim is made on a package of cookies

---

1 Department of Justice Canada. *Food and Drugs Act.* "Food and Drug Regulations,"
   Table following B.01.513(11).
2 Department of Justice Canada. *Food and Drugs Act.* "Food and Drug Regulations,"
   Schedule M(8).

that declares a serving size of 20 grams on the nutrition facts table, the food would have to contain less than 0.5 grams of fat per 20-gram serving, but also per the 30-gram reference amount.

 Did you know?

All nutrient content claims have prescribed wording that must be used, and within this prescribed wording are options. For example, "Fat-Free" can also be stated as "Free of Fat," "No Fat," "0 Fat," "Zero Fat," "Without Fat," "Contains No Fat," and "Non-Fat." Other wording, such as "Minimal Fat," "Sensible Fat," and "Not a Lot of Fat," is not permitted to be used on food labels to describe the absence or abundance of a nutrient.

☑ Quick Tip: Although some may consider nutrient content claims, such as fat-free, to be no more than marketing ploys, they are intended to make it easier for consumers to understand key nutrient information at a glance. Food companies know, however, that they can also influence consumer purchasing behaviour. For this reason, it is still important for you to check the full nutrition facts table to ensure that all key nutrients are within your target ranges.

The Grey Areas: How Food Companies Bend the Rules

Although nutrient content claims are highly regulated, there are still a number of ways food companies try to bend the rules, and there are a number of loopholes and inconsistencies within the regulations. The following are five grey areas that set consumers up to potentially be misled:

1. Nutrient-free claims on products that don't contain the nutrient anyway.
2. Making quantitative claims when products do not qualify for nutrient content claims.
3. A loophole where "No Trans Fat" actually means "a little bit of trans fat."
4. No sugar added claims for products that still have a high sugars content or that contain artificial sweeteners.
5. The multiple interpretations of the claim "Light."

Nutrition Claim Grey Area 1: Nutrient-Free Claims on Products That Don't Contain the Nutrient Anyway

Nutrient content claims are often displayed on products that typically do not contain a specific nutrient. For example, fat-free claims on candy products that are usually made from sugar, colour, and flavour, and thus almost never have any fat in the first place. You may end up buying the product with the fat-free claim over the one beside it, when both products contain virtually the same ingredients. Companies know that consumers are looking for appealing claims on their labels; therefore, they can get away with displaying just about any nutrient content claim as long as the ingredients required to yield the nutrients are allowed in the food and the product meets the requirements to make the claim.

Using the example above, candy is an unstandardized product (i.e., it does not have to meet any specific requirements for the ingredients it can and cannot contain [with the exception of additives]). Therefore, although candy typically does not contain oils or fats, in essence, it could, and although a fat-free claim is potentially misleading, it is still allowed as long as the food contains less than the regulated requirement of "less than 0.5 grams of fat per reference amount and per serving size as stated on the nutrition facts table."[3]

Canned fruit, on the other hand, is a standardized product, and therefore all of the ingredients permitted in canned fruit are defined in the Food and Drug Regulations and Processed Products Regulations. The regulation for canned fruit does not allow for fats and oils to be added as optional ingredients;[4] therefore, it would be against the rules to place a fat-free nutrient content claim on a canned fruit product unless it was further qualified with a statement such as "All Canned Fruits Are Fat-Free."[5]

When a standardized food is allowed to have oils or fats added, even in products that you wouldn't normally expect to find vegetable oils (such as pickles, relishes, and chutneys[6]), a fat-free claim is perfectly legitimate if the food contains less than 0.5 grams of fat per reference amount and per serving size stated on the nutrition facts table.

---

3 Department of Justice Canada. *Food and Drugs Act.* "Food and Drug Regulations," Table following B.01.513(11).
4 Department of Justice Canada. *Food and Drugs Act.* "Food and Drug Regulations," B.11.101. [S].
5 Department of Justice Canada. *Food and Drugs Act.* "Food and Drug Regulations," B.01.511(4).
6 Department of Justice Canada. *Canadian Agricultural Products Act.* "Processed Products Regulations," Schedule II(38).

Did you know?

There can be danger lurking in fat-free foods! Fat as an ingredient in foods generally makes a food taste better by contributing to flavour and how the food feels in the mouth. I'm sure you will agree that there is a difference between vegetables cooked with butter and vegetables steamed in water.

Always check the sugars and sodium levels on the nutrition facts table. You may be surprised to find that they are higher than the regular full-fat product. This is often done to make up for the loss in flavour. Take note of the additives that have been added to the product to compensate for characteristics such as mouth feel, texture, and shelf life.

Other examples of misleading nutrient content claims you may find on products may include the following:

- The claim "Cholesterol-Free" displayed on French fry and vegetable oil labels. All vegetables, including potatoes, and all vegetable oils are inherently free of cholesterol.
- The claim "Trans Fat–Free" displayed on vegetable oil labels. All vegetable oils in their natural states are inherently free of trans fats.
- The claim "Low in Fat" displayed on pasta labels. Just about all conventional pastas on the market are made with wheat flour or whole-wheat flour that has potentially been combined with vitamins and minerals. Therefore, the amount of fat declared on

the nutrition facts table is the amount of fat that is naturally occurring in the wheat or whole-wheat flour, which almost always ranges from 1 gram to 2 grams, depending on the serving size declared and based on a reference amount of 85 grams.[7] Be aware that pasta products made with the addition of eggs, such as egg noodles or egg pasta, typically do not meet the requirements to make the claim "Low in Fat" because of the addition of whole eggs.

Similar to the canned fruit example on page 121, it is now necessary for these types of claims to be further qualified so that consumers understand that none of the types of foods they are displayed on contain the nutrients highlighted. For example, a "Cholesterol-Free" claim on French fries would have to be further qualified with a statement similar to "All French Fries Are Cholesterol-Free Foods."[8]

☑ Quick Tip: Be aware that just because a product meets the criteria for fat-free does not mean the product is healthful.

Nutrition Claim Grey Area 2: Making Quantitative Claims When Products Do Not Qualify for Nutrient Content Claims

When a food company wants to emphasize the actual amount of a nutrient per serving size stated on the label, they can display what is called a *quantitative declaration*, which is simply stating information (facts)

---

7 Department of Justice Canada. *Food and Drugs Act.* "Food and Drug Regulations," Schedule M(35).
8 Department of Justice Canada. *Food and Drugs Act.* "Food and Drug Regulations," B.01.511(4).

found on the nutrition facts table. For example, if a product contained 2 grams of fibre per 50-gram serving, a quantitative claim may read "2 g Fibre per 50 g Serving."[9] In my experience, food companies typically use quantitative claims when foods do not meet the requirements to make nutrient content claims.

It is not uncommon for food companies to try to emphasize key words as part of quantitative claims (e.g., "fibre," "omega-3," "vitamin C"). Words may be emphasized by making them bigger or brighter or setting them in bold. Although food companies try to push the limits, the rules clearly state that all words, numbers, signs, and symbols that are part of a claim must be of the same size and prominence.[10]

I recently came across a label that declared "0.1 g Omega-3 Polyunsaturated Fat per 250 mL Serving." In Canada, a food must contain 0.3 grams or more of omega-3 polyunsaturated fat per reference amount and per serving size stated on the nutrition facts table in order to make a nutrient claim highlighting omega-3.[11] I believe that food companies use quantitative claims, such as the claim above, for two reasons:

1. In hopes that consumers will not have an understanding of what constitutes an ideal or perhaps beneficial amount of a specific nutrient.

2. So that they are able to add key words to their labels that will attract consumers to their products (e.g., "omega-3").

---

9 Department of Justice Canada. *Food and Drugs Act.* "Food and Drug Regulations," B.01.301.

10 Department of Justice Canada. *Food and Drugs Act.* "Food and Drug Regulations," B.01.503(3).

11 Department of Justice Canada. *Food and Drugs Act.* "Food and Drug Regulations," Table following B.01.513(25).

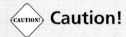 **Caution!**

When quantitative claims are made on labels, the information pertains only to the serving size stated on the nutrition facts table. The reference amounts, which I mentioned earlier that help to ensure consistency across food categories, are no longer applicable.

Nutrition Claim Grey Area 3: A Loophole Where "No Trans Fat" Actually Means "a Little Bit of Trans Fat"

Trans fats have never been as top of mind for consumers as they are today, and yet we still find ingredients contributing high levels of trans fats to the prepackaged processed foods we find at our local stores. Although many health experts recommend that our daily intake of trans fat be as close to zero grams as possible, the Food and Drug Regulations stipulate that to make the claim "No Trans Fat," –

1. a food must contain less than 0.2 grams of trans fat per reference amount and per the serving size stated on the nutrition facts table, *and*

2. the food must contain 2 grams or less of saturated fat and trans fat combined per reference amount and serving size stated on the nutrition facts table, *and*

3. the food must contain 15 per cent or less of energy from the sum of saturated fat and trans fat.[12]

---

12 Department of Justice Canada. *Food and Drugs Act.* "Food and Drug Regulations," Table following B.01.513(22).

The requirements may seem confusing, but what they really mean is that a food can contain some trans fat, even though a "No Trans Fat" claim appears on the label.

 Did you know?

Although the claim "Contains a Little Trans Fat" may be more appropriate, the following prescribed wording must be used for claims that meet the requirements for no trans fat: "Free of Trans Fat,"* "Trans Fat–Free,"* "No Trans Fat,"* "0 Trans Fat,"* "Zero Trans Fat,"* "Without Trans Fat,"* "Contains No Trans Fat," or "Contains No Trans Fatty Acids."†

* Note: The text "trans fat" can be replaced with "trans fatty acids" or "trans" on labels.

† Department of Justice Canada. *Food and Drugs Act.* "Food and Drug Regulations," Table following B.01.513(22).

Let's look at an example. I worked on a label for a cookie product some time ago that contained 0.19 grams of trans fat per 30 grams (the reference amount and serving size stated in the nutrition facts table on the label). In the case of these specific cookies, that translated into five small cookies. The first ingredient in the cookies was "hydrogenated vegetable oil." As noted in the "Caution" box on page 127, the word *hydrogenated* is a dead giveaway that a product contains trans fat. However, because food companies are permitted to label trans fat as 0 grams when a food contains less than 0.2 grams of trans

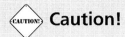 # Caution!

If the following words are found in the list of ingredients on a product with a "No Trans Fat" claim, the amount of trans fat is more than likely closer to 0.2 grams than 0 grams per serving:

- Hydrogenated
- Partially hydrogenated (the word partially is not permitted in Canada to describe hydrogenated oils, but you may still find it in the list of ingredients)
- Shortening
- Margarine (if it contains hydrogenated or partially hydrogenated oils)

The following foods (not an all-inclusive list) have been known to contain trans fat; be sure to look at the amount of trans fat declared on the nutrition facts table per serving size:

- Margarine products
- Snack foods such as crackers and potato chips
- Baked goods such as cookies, doughnuts, cakes, muffins, and breads
- Fried foods such as chicken and fish, especially when breaded or wrapped in pastry
- Beef, lamb, and some dairy products that contain naturally occurring trans fats

fat per serving,[13] the cookies snuck by and were permitted to declare the trans fat value as a deceiving 0 grams on the nutrition facts table.

In this case, there may not be much concern if you ate one serving of five small cookies; however, the cumulative effect of eating two or three times the serving size (or the whole box, as some have been known to do) may be of greater concern, especially when added to any other food with low or trace amounts of trans fat that you may have consumed over the course of the day. These small amounts can quickly add up to higher levels that may be outside of your desired range.

 Caution!

The *New England Journal of Medicine* reported that consuming as little as 1 gram of trans fat a day will increase your risk of cardiovascular disease by 20 per cent.*

* Hu FB, Stampfer MJ, Manson JE, et al. Dietary fat intake and the risk of coronary heart disease in women. *N Engl J Med.* 1997; 337(21):1491–1499.

---

13 The food must also contain 2 grams or less of saturated fatty acids and trans fatty acids combined per reference amount and serving of stated size, and the food must provide 15 per cent or less energy from the sum of saturated fatty acids and trans fatty acids. If these condition were not met, the trans fat value would have to of been declared as 0.2 g trans fatty acids and a trans fat–free claim could not appear on the label. Department of Justice Canada. *Food and Drugs Act.* "Food and Drug Regulations," Table following B.01.513(22).

(✓) Quick Tip

Look out for the descriptions "non-hydrogenated" or "partially hydrogenated" in the list of ingredients. Food companies use these descriptions to mislead consumers into thinking their products contain no or little trans fat; however, it's possible that they may still contain some trans fat, as well as high amounts of fat, saturated fat, and cholesterol, which may be of concern to you.

Although the description "non-hydrogenated" is permitted if truthful, the CFIA typically discourages descriptive information from appearing within the list of ingredients as it may mislead consumers.[14] The description "partially hydrogenated" is not permitted to appear as part of ingredient names on labels in Canada;[15] however, it is permitted in the United States; therefore, you still may find it on your labels. Always refer back to the nutrition facts table for the trans fat information.

Don't Despair ...

Today, as a result of government and consumer pressure to reduce the amount of trans fat in foods found in the Canadian market, many food companies have reformulated products. For the most part, trans fats (hydrogenated oils) have been removed from products and replaced with saturated fats and more healthful unsaturated fats. Keep in mind, however, that although potentially less harmful than trans

---

14 Canadian Food Inspection Agency. "Decisions: Ingredients List," January 2, 2007, www.inspection.gc.ca/english/fssa/labeti/decisions/ingrede.shtml.
15 Department of Justice Canada. *Food and Drugs Act.* "Food and Drug Regulations," B.01.010(3)(a)(14 & 15).

fat, consuming high quantities of saturated and unsaturated fats should still be of concern to Canadians.

 Did you know?

It is not uncommon to see the ingredient "modified vegetable oil" in products that used to contain "hydrogenated vegetable oil." Vegetable oils that have been modified by the complete or partial removal of a fatty acid must be labelled as "modified vegetable oil" or with the word *modified* preceding the actual name of the vegetable oil (e.g., "modified palm oil").* Rest assured that modified oils are not the same as hydrogenated oils (trans fats), which must still be labelled as "hydrogenated vegetable oil" or with the word *hydrogenated* preceding the actual name of the vegetable oil (e.g., "hydrogenated palm oil")† within the list of ingredients.

* Department of Justice Canada. *Food and Drugs Act.* "Food and Drug Regulations," B.01.010(3)(a)(17 & 18).

† Department of Justice Canada. *Food and Drugs Act.* "Food and Drug Regulations," B.01.101(3)(a)(14 & 15).

☑ Quick Tips

- Remember that some products that display a trans fat amount of 0 grams per serving, and claim to be trans fat–free, may actually contain upwards of 0.2 grams of trans fat per serving.
- Always compare the amount of trans fat specified in the nutrition facts table with the serving size. If you are consuming two, three, or four times the serving size specified,

take into account the amount of trans fat you are actually consuming.

- Be sure not to confuse "trans fat–free" with "fat-free." Just because a product claims to be trans fat–free does not mean it is fat-free. Remember to always check the amount of fat in the product.

- Unfortunately, at the present time it is not mandatory for restaurants to disclose the amount of trans fat present in their dishes. If a nutritional analysis is not available, some general tips for dining out include the following: Avoid deep-fried dishes unless the restaurant can confirm that the oil is non-hydrogenated, and avoid pastries and baked goods that may have been prepared using vegetable shortening, hydrogenated margarines, or hydrogenated oils.

Nutrition Claim Grey Area 4: No Sugar Added Claims for Products That Still Have a High Sugars Content

Have you ever picked up a product with the claim "No Sugar Added," "No Added Sugar," or "Without Added Sugar" and noticed that the product's nutrition facts table shows that there are still well over 20 grams of sugars per serving?

The claim "No Sugar Added" is commonly misused by food companies and is almost always displayed on products containing fruits that are already naturally high in sugars, such as fruit juices, fruit jams and spreads, and canned fruit. It is extremely important to always check the amount of sugars on the nutrition facts table, even when you see this claim.

For a food to display the claim "No Sugar Added," the following rules apply:[16]

1. It is not permitted to contain any added sugars or any ingredients that contain added sugars.
2. It is not permitted to contain ingredients that contain sugars that may functionally substitute for added sugars.
3. The sugars content cannot be increased through some other means except if the functional effect is not to increase the sugars content of the food.
4. A similar reference food must contain added sugars.

Talk about technical regulatory lingo!

The first part of the claim requirements seems pretty straightforward; if a "No Sugar Added" claim was displayed on a label, one would immediately assume that the food could not contain any added sugars.

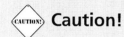 **Caution!**

When sugars are declared in the list of ingredients using the word *sugar*, they are easy to identify; however, there are many less-assuming sources of sugar that can be found in the lists of ingredients of your favourite prepackaged processed foods. Refer back to the table "Twenty-Five Common Ingredient Names for Sugar" in chapter 9 for a list of ingredient names to look out for.

---

16 Department of Justice Canada. *Food and Drugs Act.* "Food and Drug Regulations," Table following B.01.513(40).

We are then further protected by the three additional stipulations noted on page 132 which, when translated, mean the following:

1. The food cannot contain ingredients such as fruit juices, concentrated fruit juices, and/or apple sauce that contain high amounts of sugars that have been added to the food specifically to sweeten it. For example, baked goods that contain fruit juices and concentrated fruit juices that act as sweetening substitutes for white sugar would not be permitted to display the claim "No Sugar Added."

2. If apple sauce is added to impart an apple flavour to a food and not increase the sweetness, or if fruit juices are added to impart a flavour and not further sweeten the product, a "No Sugar Added" claim would be acceptable. Look for an indication that the fruit juice or purée has been added for flavouring purposes. For example, a fruit spread with concentrated apple juice added for flavouring purposes may be labelled "Strawberry and Concentrated Apple Juice Spread."

3. There must be a similar food to the food that is making the "No Sugar Added" claim on the market that contains added sugars. For example, the claim "No Sugar Added" can be displayed on a label for a 100 per cent orange juice product because sugar is permitted to be added to orange juice, and some orange juice products on the market contain sugar. A "No Sugar Added" claim could not be displayed, however, on a product that was not permitted to contain sugar, such as apple juice, butter, and vegetable oils.[17]

---

17 Department of Justice Canada. *Food and Drugs Act.* "Food and Drug Regulations," B.11.123. [S], B.08.056. [S], and B.09.001. [S].

Be aware that "sugar" and "sweeteners" are not the same thing. Products that do not contain added sugars but do contain added artificial sweeteners such as aspartame, acesulfame-potassium, and sucralose still qualify to make the "No Sugar Added" claim.

If you are concerned about your sugars intake, products that display the claim "Unsweetened" are the way to go! "Unsweetened" is a regulated claim that is only permitted to appear on labels when a food meets the requirements for the claim "No Sugar Added," and also does not contain any sweeteners such as artificial sweeteners or sugar alcohols.[18]

 Caution!

Claims such as "Does Not Taste Sweet" are not considered nutrient content claims; therefore, they do not have to meet specific requirements to be displayed on a label. Although claims highlighting sensory attributes are not permitted to be misleading and untruthful, I recommend that you read them with a grain of salt, since what constitutes a "sweet taste" is subjective. Always check the sugars amount on the nutrition facts table per the serving size stated to understand how much sugar you are about to consume. If the product does not fall within your desired range, leave it on the shelf.

18 Department of Justice Canada. *Food and Drugs Act*. "Food and Drug Regulations," B.01.509.

☑ Quick Tips

- Always check the sugars amount on the nutrition facts table. Remember to always check the amount as it relates to the serving size.
- Look for fruit that is packed in water, not syrup. This is the only type of canned fruit product that qualifies to make the "No Sugar Added" claim. If you are concerned about artificial sweeteners, make sure you read the list of ingredients.
- Look for the claim "Unsweetened" to guarantee that no added sugars or sweeteners (including artificial sweeteners and/or sugar alcohols) have been added to the product.

Nutrition Claim Grey Area 5:
The Multiple Interpretations of "Light"

The claim "Light" is commonly found on products such as margarine, jam, juice, maple syrup, tuna, olive oil, and potato chips. I believe the first thing most consumers think of when they see the claim "Light" on a food label is that the product is low or reduced in calories, and therefore potentially more healthful than a similar product. There are actually four meanings for the word *light* when incorporated into claims on labels, and it is important to understand each of them and to think about how they can be interchanged, so that you are not misled.

The Four Different Meanings for the Claim "Light"

Version of Light	Regulation
1. Light as in "Light in Energy" plus a qualifying statement	at least 25% fewer calories[19]
2. Light as in "Light in Fat" plus a qualifying statement	at least 25% less fat[20]
3. Light as in "Lightly Salted" plus a qualifying statement	at least 50% less salt[21]
4. Light as is "Light in Colour" or "Light in Texture"	no standard of measure

19 The food is processed, formulated, reformulated, or otherwise modified so that it provides at least 25 per cent less energy per reference amount of the food than the reference amount of the similar reference food. The similar reference food does not meet the conditions set out in column 2 of item 2 for the subject "low in energy" (the food provides 40 calories or 167 kilojoules or less per reference amount and serving of stated size and, in the case of a food other than a table-top sweetener, if the reference amount is 30 g or 30 mL or less per 50 g). Department of Justice Canada. *Food and Drugs Act.* "Food and Drug Regulations," Table following B.01.513(45).

20 The food is processed, formulated, reformulated, or otherwise modified so that it contains at least 25 per cent less fat per reference amount of the food than the reference amount of the similar reference food. The similar reference food does not meet the conditions for the claim "Low in Fat" (the food contains 3 g or less of fat per reference amount and serving of stated size and, if the reference amount is 30 g or 30 mL or less per 50 g). Department of Justice Canada. *Food and Drugs Act.* "Food and Drug Regulations," Table following B.01.513(45).

21 The food contains at least 50 per cent less added sodium than the sodium added to the similar reference food, and the similar reference food does not meet the conditions for the claim "Low in Sodium or Salt" (the food contains 140 mg or less of sodium per reference amount and serving of stated size and, if the reference amount is 30 g or 30 mL or less, per 50 g). Department of Justice Canada. *Food and Drugs Act.* "Food and Drug Regulations," Table following B.01.513(36).

When manufacturers want to compare nutritionally altered products with regular products, the claim "Light" is permitted to describe a 25 per cent reduction in energy (calories)[22] or a 25 per cent reduction in fat.[23] Let's look at two examples:

1. Brand X regular strawberry jam may contain 100 calories per serving, whereas Brand X light strawberry jam may contain 70 calories per serving. In this case, the label of Brand X light strawberry jam may read "Light – 30% Fewer Calories than Brand X Regular Strawberry Jam."

2. Brand X regular margarine may contain 10 grams of fat per serving, whereas Brand X light margarine may contain 5 grams of fat per serving. In this case, the label on Brand X light margarine may read "Light – 50% Less Fat than Brand X Regular Margarine."

When manufacturers want to compare products that have been reformulated to contain 50 per cent less sodium, they are permitted to use the claims "Lightly Salted" or "Salted Lightly";[24] for example, –

• Brand X regular potato chips may contain 500 mg of sodium per serving, whereas Brand X lightly salted potato chips may contain 200 mg of sodium per serving. In this case, the label of Brand X lightly salted potato chips may read "Lightly Salted – 60% Less Sodium than Brand X Regular Potato Chips."

22 Department of Justice Canada. *Food and Drugs Act.* "Food and Drug Regulations," Table following B.01.513(45).

23 Ibid.

24 Department of Justice Canada. *Food and Drugs Act.* "Food and Drug Regulations," Table following B.01.513(36).

Did you know?

Foods that are typically high in sodium may include canned soups, canned vegetables, condiments such as barbeque sauce and soy sauce, dehydrated soup and sauce mixes, processed meats, processed cheeses, crackers, breads, potato chips, and frozen entrées. Look for claims such as "Lightly Salted," followed by a qualifying statement indicating the sodium level has been reduced in these types of foods.

 Caution!

Just because a product makes the claim "Light in Calories," "Light in Fat," or "Lightly Salted" does not always mean the amount of calories, fat, or sodium is as low as you may think. All three claims are based on comparisons with similar products that may be very high in calories, fat, and salt. Twenty-five per cent less fat of an extremely high amount is still a lot of fat. Always refer to the nutrition facts table for the actual amount of calories, fat, and sodium the product contains, as well as the per cent daily values, and compare these amounts with the recommendations made by your health-care provider.

Label reading can become a little tricky when the claim "Light" is used to describe the sensory characteristics of a food, such as the colour or texture. Although, it is perfectly legal for food companies to display the word *light* accompanied by a qualifying statement describing the characteristic such as "Light in Colour" or "Light in Texture,"[25] these claims do not relate to the nutrient content of the food at all.

 Caution!

Look out for the claim "Light in Taste." Although taste may be loosely related to a sensory characteristic, taste may imply an ideal level of healthfulness. The claim "Light in Taste" is not regulated, meaning the food does not have to meet specific nutrient requirements to display the claim (other than not being misleading), and should therefore be read with a grain of salt.

Although the regulations may seem complex enough up to this point, the following three products add another level of complexity:

1. The terms *light* and *extra-light* as they relate to maple syrup are regulated and representative of colour classes, or to be more specific, the percentage of light transmission through the syrup.[26] Do not be misled by these words on maple syrup labels; they are not representative of lower-calorie products.

---

25 Canadian Food Inspection Agency. *Guide to Food Labelling and Advertising*, Section 3.7.2.
26 Department of Justice Canada. *Canada Agricultural Products Act.* "Maple Products Regulations," Schedule III(2).

2. It is common practice for food companies to display the terms *light* and *extra-light* on olive oil labels as they relate to colour. Do not be misled by these words; they are not representative of lower-fat oils. All olive oils contain approximately 120 calories and 13.5 grams of fat in a 1 tablespoon serving.[27]

3. Be warned that the indications "Light Meat Tuna" and "Light Tuna" found on cans of tuna do not refer to lower-calorie, lower-fat, or lower-sodium products, but instead refer to "canned tuna that has a diffuse luminous reflectance of not less than 22.6 per cent that of magnesium oxide."[28]

✓ Quick Tip: The claim "Light" is no longer permitted to stand alone. Always look for the qualifying or descriptive statements that must accompany "Light" claims when reading food labels. If you cannot find a qualifying or descriptive statement, always refer to the nutrition facts table to assess and compare calorie and nutrient amounts. Remember to always check and compare the serving size as well.

---

27 Health Canada. "Canadian Nutrient File: Vegetable Oil, Olive." Food Code: 422.

28 Department of Justice Canada. *Fish Inspection Act.* "Fish Inspection Regulations," Part IV, Canned Fish (49)(b).

❓ Did you know?

"Light Syrup" is a common statement that you will find on canned and frozen fruit labels. Canned and frozen fruits are permitted to be packed in water, fruit juice or fruit juice from concentrate, slightly sweetened water or slightly sweetened fruit juice, light syrup or light fruit juice syrup, heavy syrup or heavy fruit juice syrup, and extra-heavy syrup or extra-heavy fruit juice syrup.* Unfortunately, this statement does not represent the number of calories in the product, but instead represents the concentration of the syrup that the fruit has been packed in. For example, light syrup must contain less than 18 per cent but not less than 14 per cent soluble solids for canned fruit cocktail, peaches, pears, and mandarin oranges.† Although this may not mean much to you, what you should know is that the amount of sugars in the product will be shown in the nutrition facts table per serving. If the amount of sugars is higher than you want to consume per serving, consider leaving the product on the shelf and buying fresh fruit or canned fruit packed in water instead.

* Department of Justice Canada. *Canada Agricultural Products Act.* "Processed Products Regulations," Schedule IV, Table III.

† Department of Justice Canada. *Canada Agricultural Products Act.* "Processed Products Regulations," Schedule IV, Table III, Column IV(2).

The Inside Scoop

Visit the "Inside Scoop" page at www.grainofsalt.ca and type in the password KNOWLEDGE to gain access. Under the "Claims" section, look for a full list of many of the most popular nutrient content claims and their requirements, as per the *Food and Drugs Act*, "Food and Drug Regulations," Table following B.01.513, and the Canadian Food Inspection Agency's *Guide to Food Labelling and Advertising*, Section 7.25, Table 7–14, including the following:

- Fat claims
- Trans fat claims
- Saturated fat claims
- Omega-3 and -6 polyunsaturated fat claims
- Cholesterol claims
- Sodium claims
- Sugar claims
- Dietary fibre claims
- Vitamin and mineral claims

CHAPTER 14

Meaningless "Made with" Claims

HAVE YOU EVER PICKED UP A PREPACKAGED processed food product that made the claim "Made with Natural Ingredients" only to see artificial flavours and synthetic additives declared in the list of ingredients? How about reading the claim "Made from Whole Grains" and then finding wheat flour, which is refined and does not contain whole grains, declared as the first ingredient?

 Did you know?

Whole grains are cereal grains that contain the bran, germ, and endosperm, and are therefore nutritionally superior to refined grains that contain only the endosperm. Whole grains are generally higher in dietary fibre, antioxidants, protein, dietary minerals, and vitamins as compared with refined grains.

I am a strong advocate of healthful eating, and one of the fundamentals of healthful eating is choosing whole, natural foods that are devoid of refined and synthetic ingredients, such as additives, flavour enhancers, and artificial flavours. The claims used by food companies such as "Natural," "All Natural," "100% Whole Grains," and "100% Fruit Juice" can therefore be very powerful marketing tools that help identify the foods you are looking for.

The regulations that allow food companies to make the claim "All Natural" on their prepackaged processed food products are very strict. The product must contain 100 per cent natural ingredients to be called all natural. Obviously, foods that contain synthetic ingredients such as additives, artificial flavours, and flavour enhancers are not permitted to claim they are all natural; in addition, foods that contain ingredients that have been significantly altered from their original states (e.g., removal of caffeine, bleaching, smoking, and hydrogenation) are also excluded from the all-natural list.[1]

 Caution!

Use of synthetic pesticides, GMOs (genetically modified organisms), and other environmental contaminants are not taken into consideration when claims such as "All Natural" or "Made with Natural Ingredients" are displayed on food labels in Canada. The word *natural* indicates that ingredients are from natural sources versus synthetic or artificial sources. If you are concerned with GMOs and synthetic

---

1 Canadian Food Inspection Agency. *Guide to Food Labelling and Advertising*, Section 4.7.

pesticides, buy organic! Foods certified as organic are free of synthetic pesticides and synthetic growth regulators (including hormones), and they cannot be genetically engineered, irradiated, or from cloned animals (with exceptions).*

* Canadian General Standards Board. *Organic Production Systems General Principles and Management Standards* 1.4, "Prohibited Substances, Methods or Ingredients in Organic Production and Handling." CAN/CGSB-32.310-2006, amended October 2008, and *Organic Products Systems Permitted Substances Lists*, CAN/CGSB-32.311-2006, amended August 2011.

 ## The Inside Scoop

Visit the "Inside Scoop" page at www.grainofsalt.ca and type in the password KNOWLEDGE to gain access. Under the "All Things Organic" section look for more information on organic regulations in Canada.

The regulations for highlighting desirable ingredients found in prepackaged processed foods are a little more straightforward and typically require the percentage of the highlighted ingredient to be displayed. For example, "100% Whole Grains," "100% Whole Wheat," or "100% Real Fruit Juice" are common claims you may find on prepackaged processed food labels.

The Grey Areas: How Food Companies Bend the Rules

Using statements such as "Made with ...," "Made from...," and "Contains ..." allows food companies to highlight superior ingredients found in prepackaged processed foods in varying amounts. Although these claims must be truthful, they do not have to meet any specific minimum requirements for the amount of the ingredient that must actually be in the product. For example, claims such as "100% Natural Ingredients," "100% Whole Grains," or "100% Fruit Juice" are often substituted with statements such as "Contains Natural Ingredients," "Made from Whole Grains," or "Contains Fruit Juice," when the food does not meet the 100 per cent requirement. These claims are ambiguous; just about any prepackaged processed food that contains at least one natural ingredient or one whole grain can use these claims. However, does the product contain a total of 1 per cent of the desired ingredient or 99 per cent of the desired ingredient?

✓ **Quick Tip: When you read claims starting with the words "Made with" and "Contains," it is a good idea to check the list of ingredients to confirm the relative presence of the highlighted ingredient in the food. Remember that the ingredients found in the product in the greatest amount are listed first. Also, keep in mind that if the ingredient that is highlighted is present in the product in a significant amount, it would most likely be accompanied by a per cent declaration such as "Contains 60% Whole Grains" or "Made with 50% Fruit Juice."**

Let's look at a few examples. The following cookie product displays the claims "Made with Natural Ingredients" and "Made from Whole Wheat" on its label:

- Ingredients: enriched wheat flour, palm and modified palm oils, cocoa, sugar, whole-wheat flour, baking soda, natural flavour, sea salt, skim milk powder, soy lecithin, caramel, sodium benzoate.

Technically both claims are truthful, as this product does in fact contain some natural ingredients, such as cocoa, sea salt, and natural flavour, and it does contain whole-wheat flour. You may not want to purchase it, however, if you are looking to avoid the other modified and synthetic ingredients it contains or if you are trying to avoid refined-grain ingredients such as enriched wheat flour, which is the predominant ingredient in this product (present in the greatest amount).

How about the following fruit-flavoured candy product that displays the claim "Made with Fruit Juice"?

- Ingredients: corn syrup, sugar/glucose-fructose, modified corn starch, citric acid, sodium citrate, fruit juice from concentrate (apple, grape, raspberry), artificial flavour, colour.

The product does in fact contain real fruit juice; however, it also contains artificial flavours, colour (which more than likely includes some artificial colours), and some additives that are present in the product in a greater amount than the fruit juice.

☑ Quick Tip: As a general rule of thumb, it is almost always safe to assume that, because most additives comprise less than 2 per cent of the total of a product's formulation (recipe of ingredients), ingredients listed after additives are declared in the list of ingredients are typically not present in significant amounts.

Finally, as discussed previously, recall the potentially misleading ways that food companies develop brand names to entice consumers. The next time you are in the grocery store, keep your eyes open and you will be surprised how often you see the word *natural*, or a derivative of the word natural, in a product's trademark or brand name.

Empower Yourself!

1. Be skeptical of claims starting with the words "Made from ...," "Made with ...," and "Contains ...," as most prepackaged processed foods can easily contain some desired ingredients, but they may also contain other less desirable ingredients, such as artificial, synthetic, and refined ingredients.

2. Always check the list of ingredients and look for where the desired ingredients are listed. Does it appear that the desired ingredients are closer to 5 per cent or 95 per cent of the product?

3. When considering prepackaged processed foods based on highlighted desirable attributes, always look for a 100 per cent statement or another factual statement confirming a specific percentage, such as "100% Whole Wheat," "75% Whole Grains," or "50% Fruit Juice." Keep in mind that it may be safe to assume that the amount of a highlighted ingredient may be lower than your desired level if a specific percentage is not declared on the label.

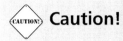 **Caution!**

Whole-wheat bread does not always contain 100 per cent whole-wheat flour. Whole-wheat bread is a standardized food, and as per the Food and Drug Regulations, it can contain between 60 per cent and 100 per cent whole-wheat flour.* This means it is possible that your whole-wheat bread contains 60 per cent whole-wheat flour and 40 per cent refined-wheat flour. The percentage of whole-wheat flour must accompany the name of the product; therefore, *always* look for the indication 100 per cent as part of the name "Whole-Wheat Bread."

Also be aware that whole-wheat bread is permitted to contain caramel. Caramel may be added to whole-wheat bread to give it a nice brown colour that may trick consumers into thinking the bread is more healthful than it may be. Remember to check the per cent of whole-wheat flour declared on the front of the label, and check the nutrition facts table to ensure the bread contains the amount of fibre you are looking for per serving.

* Department of Justice Canada. *Food and Drugs Act.* "Food and Drug Regulations," B.13.026. [S].

CHAPTER 15

Ten Additional Claims to Look Out For

ONE OF THE MAIN REASONS WHY CLAIMS on food labels are so confusing is that the average consumer may not have an understanding of which claims are regulated (have to meet specific requirements) and which are not (simply have to be truthful). We depend on the government to protect us by allowing food companies to place regulated, consistent claims on our labels, and we look for these claims. What happens, however, is that food companies figure out how to bend the rules and exploit the "grey areas," and what we are left with are truthful yet potentially misleading claims that may convince the average consumer to buy products that don't actually have all of the attributes they were looking for.

Look out for the following ten claims when you are shopping. **Remember that there is no quick and easy way to decipher food labels.** Claims are displayed on labels to try to persuade you to buy products; however, as an insider, you now know that it is important to read the ingredient and nutrition information so that you are able to properly interpret the claims.

1. "100% Wheat"
   - This claim highlights that a product contains 100 per cent refined wheat and does not refer to whole grains or whole wheat at all. Refined wheat, predominantly found in white bread, crackers, cereal bars, breakfast cereals, cookies, and other baked goods, does not have the same nutritional profile as whole wheat or whole grains. Always look for the word *whole* as part of the claim, part of the product name, or within the list of ingredients.

2. "Multigrain"
   - This claim simply refers to the types of grains that are in a product (e.g., corn, wheat, rye, barley, oats, and rice). This claim does not confirm if these grains are whole (e.g., wheat vs. whole wheat, or white rice vs. whole-grain brown rice). Always look for an additional statement such as "100% Whole Grain" to accompany the claim "Multigrain." If you cannot find a whole-grain statement, look for the word *whole* within the list of ingredients.

3. "# grams Whole Grains per Serving"
   - Do not confuse whole grains with fibre. Adding or increasing the amount of whole grains found in foods typically increases the amount of fibre found in the food. The number of whole grains found in the food per serving does not, however, equal the number of grams of fibre per serving. A perfect example is a product I recently found in my local grocery store that displayed the claim "8 g Whole Grains per Serving" on the front

of its label, but it contained only 2 grams of fibre per serving when I checked the nutrition facts table.

4. "Lightly Sweetened," "Lightly Seasoned," and "Lightly Breaded"

   • When the word *lightly* is used in a claim, it implies that only a small amount of the ingredient (e.g., sugar, seasoning [in this case, seasoning should be interpreted to mean salt to be safe], and breading) has been added to the food. These claims are not regulated, meaning they do not have to meet specific requirements regarding the amount of sugars or salt or breading used. Always check the nutrition facts table for the actual amounts of nutrients you may be concerned with.

5. "Homemade Taste" and "Homemade Style"

   • When the words *taste* and *style* follow a claim, they generally imply that the attribute the food company is trying to highlight is not what it claims to be. The claims "Homemade Taste" and "Homemade Style" are typically used on products that are processed in large manufacturing facilities that are far from resembling your home kitchen. These words can also be used to manipulate claims to imply an ethnic food is authentic, when in fact it is manufactured on the opposite side of the world. Look out for the word *style* incorporated into product names such as "Swedish-Style Meatballs," "Thai-Style Coconut Soup," and "Indian-Style Curry." If the food is actually made in the country that is highlighted, the word *style* will typically not appear.

6. "The Goodness of Corn," "The Goodness of Wheat," "The Goodness of Rice"

    • The word *goodness* is typically displayed on labels so that consumers see the word *good* and think they are eating something that is good for them. There are currently no criteria for use of the word *goodness* on labels except that it cannot be misleading or untruthful. Just about all whole foods in their natural states offer us some advantages, no matter how insignificant, and thus, in theory, can be described using the word *goodness*. The problem, however, is that in most cases the ingredient has been highly processed, potentially eliminating virtually all of its goodness. It is also important to note that just because one ingredient in the product is highlighted as contributing goodness does not mean that the other ingredients do as well.

7. "Flavoured with Real Fruit"

    • The claim "Flavoured with Real Fruit" is a fancy way of saying "Natural Flavour" or "Natural Fruit Flavour." The word *real* is very appealing to consumers, and marketers know this. Natural flavours are produced from animal or vegetable raw materials, which means that all natural flavours are made from *real* food. When the claim "Flavoured with Real Fruit" is used on labels, there is a chance that a consumer may only read the text "Real Fruit" and not realize it is actually just fruit flavour. If you are looking for products that contain real fruit rather than natural fruit flavour, always check the list of ingredients.

Caution!

Some products claiming to contain real fruit may actually only contain concentrated fruit juice, or a combination of fruit and fruit juice. Be sure to read the list of ingredients to determine if the product contains a fruit purée (the real deal), concentrated fruit juice, or simply natural fruit flavour.

8. "A Touch of Sweetness"
   • Similar to the claim "Lightly Sweetened," the claim "A Touch of Sweetness" also implies that only a small amount of sugars have been added to a product. Although potentially considered misleading, this claim is most commonly found on breakfast cereal products and does not have to meet any regulatory requirements for the amount of sugars the product contains. Translation: "A Touch of Sweetness" is trying to trick you into believing the product does not contain a lot of sugar. It is up to you to judge for yourself! Check out the list of ingredients and sugars amount on the nutrition facts table. Not sure how to identify sugars in the list of ingredients? Refer back to chapter 9 for a list of twenty-five common ingredient names that, in essence, all mean sugar.

9. "Naturally Sweet Corn," "Naturally Sweet Rice," and "Naturally Sweet Wheat"
   - These claims are most commonly displayed on the front of breakfast cereal boxes. They imply that the main ingredients of the cereal (corn, rice, wheat, etc.) are responsible for imparting the sweet flavour; however, this is not always the case. One box I picked up while shopping that displayed a claim similar to these contained sugar, fancy molasses, and barley malt syrup, in addition to the naturally sweet corn, and declared a sugars amount of 3 grams per 30-gram serving (that means that 10 per cent of every serving was sugar).
10. "100% Wholesome"
    - There are currently no criteria for use of the word *wholesome* as it relates to prepackaged processed foods, which means that when the word *wholesome* is displayed, it is simply not permitted to be misleading. Wholesome, as it relates to food, typically implies that the food is healthful. One of the foods I have found this claim on contained refined wheat (no whole grains), maltodextrin, and whey protein concentrate—not exactly what comes to mind when I think of "wholesome" food. Remember that we all have different nutrient requirements, health conditions, and potential intolerances; therefore, even if a food company legitimately stands behind their product as being wholesome, it may not be a wholesome or healthful product for you.

CHAPTER 16

Country-of-Origin Statements

IN TODAY'S GLOBAL ECONOMY, WITH FOODS being sourced from all over the world, the statement "Product of Canada" is top of mind for many Canadians who are looking for locally and nationally produced foods as a source of comfort and security.

The country-of-origin statement (e.g., "Product of Canada," "Product of China," "Product of USA"), in theory, is displayed on labels to let consumers know which country the product originated from. More than likely you have picked up a product looking for the country-of-origin statement and have not been able to find one. This is not a result of an oversight by a food company, but one of the most astonishing loopholes in Canadian food labelling regulations, in which the country-of-origin statement is deemed as optional for many of the prepackaged processed food products we commonly buy, such as baked goods, breads, snack foods, some beverages, pasta products, some frozen prepared foods, breakfast cereals, and candy. Not only that, it is often common for country-of-origin statements to simply indicate the country the food was manufactured in, processed in, or shipped from, but not necessarily the country of origin of the ingredients.

?) **Did you know?**

Although it is optional to display a country-of-origin statement on many food products sold in Canada, some standardized foods such as meats, fish, dairy products, fresh fruits and vegetables, honey, and processed fruit and vegetable products have separate mandatory labelling requirements for declaring a product's country of origin.

Up until 2008, foods labelled "Product of Canada" did not necessarily have to contain any Canadian ingredients. However, after a prime-time Canadian television show let the cat out of the bag, the Canadian government was forced to appease Canadians by revising the "Product of Canada" labelling requirements.

As of December 2008, the Canadian government launched four new labelling options to communicate to consumers that a product is either made with Canadian ingredients, made with imported ingredients, made with a combination of the two, or simply processed in Canada (i.e., potentially none of the ingredients are from Canada, but the product is still processed or manufactured here).

The following are the four variations that you may find on prepackaged processed food labels:

1. "Product of Canada"
2. "Made in Canada from Domestic and Imported Ingredients"
3. "Made in Canada from Imported Ingredients"
4. "Prepared in Canada," "Processed in Canada," "Packaged in Canada," or "Refined in Canada"

Let's take a closer look. The statement "Product of Canada" can be used when all or almost all ingredients, processing, and labour used to make a food product are Canadian. This means that all significant ingredients are Canadian, and non-Canadian ingredients cannot exceed 2 per cent of the total weight of ingredients.[1]

The challenge is that given the Canadian climate, a number of core ingredients found in processed foods are not grown in Canada. Ingredients such as oranges, sugar, peanuts, vanilla, and coffee are typically grown in other countries with warmer climates.

Let's look at an example for a strawberry cereal bar:

• Ingredients: oatmeal, wheat flour, strawberries, canola oil, liquid whole egg, milk, sugar.

This product would be permitted to use the "Product of Canada" statement only if all of the major ingredients were from Canada, and the sugar, which is not a Canadian ingredient, was less than 2 per cent of the product.

If the amount of sugar was greater than 2 per cent, the "Product of Canada" statement would have to be changed to "Made in Canada from Domestic and Imported Ingredients." However, if the cereal bar was reformulated to contain Canadian honey instead of imported sugar, the statement "Product of Canada" would then be acceptable.

The statement "Made in Canada from Domestic and Imported Ingredients" is permitted to be used when a prepackaged processed food contains ingredients that are both Canadian (domestic) and

---

1 Canadian Food Inspection Agency. *Guide to Food Labelling and Advertising*, Section 4.19.1.

imported, and the food is made in Canada.[2] Similarly, the statement "Made in Canada from Imported Ingredients" is permitted to be used when the food contains 100 per cent imported ingredients, and is made in Canada.[3] Personally, neither of these statements provides me with very much comfort, as they do not provide the amount or percentage of domestic ingredients, and are thus like the meaningless "Made with ..." and "Contains ..." claims discussed in chapter 14. Are the products made with 1 per cent domestic ingredients or 99 per cent domestic ingredients? They are still worth considering, however, because it is always nice to support the Canadian economy by buying products that are made in Canada rather than products that are made in other countries and simply imported into and sold in Canada.

The Grey Areas: How Food Companies Bend the Rules

Only the statement "Product of Canada" means that the product was made in Canada with mostly (98 per cent or more) Canadian ingredients. All other country-of-origin statements that include the word Canada will have an undisclosed amount of imported ingredients.

Believe it or not, the statements "Prepared in Canada," "Processed in Canada," and "Refined in Canada" are permitted to be used without further qualification to indicate that the ingredients are a combination of Canadian and imported ingredients or simply imported ingredients.[4] These three country-of-origin variations are typically used most often

---

2 Canadian Food Inspection Agency. *Guide to Food Labelling and Advertising*, Section 4.19.2.
3 Ibid.
4 Canadian Food Inspection Agency. *Guide to Food Labelling and Advertising*, Section 4.19.3.

by food companies when their products do not qualify to the make the "Product of Canada" statement, as they are shorter (less wordy), and the taboo word *imported* does not have to be included. When you see these statements, I recommend that you err on the side of caution and assume that the products are made exclusively with imported ingredients.

 ## Caution!

Watch out for the claim "Prepared in Canada" as it reads quite simi-larly to "Product of Canada" and at a quick glance may be mistaken for the real deal.

International-Origin Statements

Although many Canadians are looking for foods made closer to home, there is still a great demand for high-quality products from countries that grow or produce superior ingredients. For example, olive oil from Italy, feta cheese from Greece, Swiss cheese from Switzerland, and Belgian chocolate from Belgium.

Food companies and importers know that consumers are looking for the real deal when it comes to these foods; therefore, they almost always highlight the country the food originated in on the front of the label. Sometimes a statement stating the product was imported from the applicable country is displayed (i.e., "Imported from Spain"), sometimes the origin of the ingredients is highlighted (i.e., "Made from Belgian Milk Chocolate"), and other times a specific country's flag is displayed.

Even though an imported prepackaged processed food product may indicate "Product of ..." followed by the country name the product was manufactured in on the label doesn't always guarantee that the ingredients in the product are actually from that country. If you are concerned with the origin of ingredients in the prepackaged processed foods you buy, I recommend that any time you see the statement "Product of ..." followed by an international country name, you read it as "Imported from ..."

Empower Yourself!

1. Take the time to look for a country-of-origin statement on your labels. The statement typically starts with the words "Product of"; however, you may also see similar versions, such as "Made in," "Processed in," and "Prepared in," followed by a country name. If you cannot find this information, check the dealer name and address information to help you determine if the food has been imported into Canada. Look for statements such as "Imported by" and "Distributed by," which may imply the product has been imported, versus "Manufactured by," which gives a clearer idea of which country the product was made in.

2. Keep in mind that in most cases, just because a food states that it was manufactured, prepared, or processed in a specific country does not necessarily mean the ingredients in the product originated from

that country. For example, cookies that declare the country-of-origin statement "Product of USA" may have simply been manufactured in the United States from ingredients that were sourced from other countries.

3. Look for terms such as *local* and *locally grown* on labels and advertisements to indicate that foods have originated within 50 kilometres of the place where they are being sold.[5]

---

5 Fresh fruits and vegetables can also make the claim "Local" if they meet the following requirements as per Department of Justice Canada's *Food and Drugs Act*, "Food and Drug Regulations," B.01.012: "Local food" means a food that is manufactured, processed, produced, or packaged in a local government unit and sold only in –
    a) the local government unit in which it is manufactured, processed, or packaged;
    b) one or more local government units that are immediately adjacent to the one in which it is manufactured, processed, produced, or packaged; or
    c) the local government unit in which it is manufactured, processed, produced, or packaged and in one or more local government units that are immediately adjacent to the one in which it is manufactured, processed, produced, or packaged.*
  * Canadian Food Inspection Agency. *Guide to Food Labelling and Advertising*. "Decisions: Claims – Composition, Quality, Quantity, and Origin: 'Local' Claim on Fresh Fruits and Vegetables," July 8, 2010, www.inspection.gc.ca/english/fssa/labeti/decisions/compoe.shtml.

CHAPTER 17

Images and Artwork

FOOD LABELS ARE LIKE WORKS OF ART. Food is all about a sensory experience, and sight is one of the senses we use to choose the foods we want to eat. Graphic designers, food stylists, and food photographers all work together as part of a food company's marketing team to create images that are provocative, enticing, and as delicious-looking as possible, while trying not to lose the true essence of the product. Little drops of water are added to images of fruits to make them look juicier; noodles and vegetables are perfectly placed on a plate and photographed to perhaps create a false impression of the package contents; and fresh, plump, and juicy fruits and vegetables appear when foods may actually contain only their dehydrated or freeze-dried counterparts.

I have to admit that I have fallen victim to trendy, sleek, delicious artwork on labels more times than I can count. We are visual people, and when you can't see or smell the food that is inside the package, all we have to go on is the picture on the label.

Images of products must accurately reflect the food that is in the package, but there are ways food companies can get away with "spicing up" these images so that they can better grab your attention while you are shopping.

The Grey Areas: How Food Companies Bend the Rules
"Serving Suggestion"

Displaying a statement similar to "Serving Suggestion" close to pictures on labels allows food companies to accompany the picture of the food in the package with other appealing foods. For example, you may be buying a prepackaged processed breakfast cereal that displays an image of the cereal topped with a variety of fresh fruit, or perhaps you are buying crackers that display an image of a cracker topped with cucumber, tomato, and cheese, potentially creating the illusion that the cracker is a healthful snack. Food companies frequently use this trick of the trade on labels to lure you in.

Adding pictures of foods to product images on labels that are not actually in the packages, regardless of the fact that the text "Serving Suggestion" has been displayed, creates potential for consumers to be misled. Although the text "Serving Suggestion" has to be displayed within close proximity to the image, it is almost always displayed in letters that are virtually impossible to read without a magnifying glass. Not only does this marketing technique potentially create a false impression of what is in the package, it may also imply the product is more healthful for you than it is in reality.

"Enlarged to Show Texture"

Images on food labels can also be enlarged, making the superior ingredients in the product appear to be more appealing than they are in reality. For example, you may find this statement on products such as the following:

- Cookies to emphasize chunks of chocolate or nuts.

- Potato chips and crackers to emphasize seasoning or crispiness.
- Products that contain cheese to emphasize how much cheese there is and how appetizing it looks when it is perfectly melted.
- Breakfast cereals to emphasize the size of the grains or superior ingredients such as nuts and dried fruits.
- Fish products to emphasize the flakiness of the fish.
- Prepared entrées and cans of soup to emphasize the individual pieces of meat or vegetables.
- Frozen pizzas to emphasize the toppings.
- Cereal bars to emphasize the fruit or fruit-flavoured filling.

As long as a statement similar to "Enlarged to Show Texture" or "Photo Enlarged" appears in close proximity to the image, food companies can get away with this trick of the trade.

Have you ever opened a package, pulled the product out, and thought "that's it?" Placing enlarged images on labels can also give you a false sense of the size of the product you are buying. You may believe cookies are larger than they actually are, or that potato chips are thicker than they really are, or even worse, that an ice cream bar is larger than it really is (a pet peeve of mine).

"Artificial Flavours"

Food companies can get away with displaying images of real foods in products that contain only artificial flavours by displaying the text "Artificially Flavoured" (or similar text) beside the images.[1] This trick

---

1 Department of Justice Canada. *Consumer Packaging and Labelling Act.* "Consumer Packaging and Labelling Regulations," 34.

of the trade is most commonly used for labels of candy products that are flavoured with artificial fruit flavours but show images of juicy fresh fruits on the label.

 Caution!

Do not let the claim "Contains Real Fruit Juice" or "Made with Real Fruit Juice" distract you from noticing the "Artificially Flavoured" claim on candy products that contain both real fruit juice and artificial flavours and show enticing images of real fruits on the label. Remember that the claims "Contains Real Fruit Juice" and "Made with Real Fruit Juice" can mean the product contains as little as a drop of fruit juice unless it is accompanied with a declaration of the amount of fruit juice the product actually contains, such as "Contains 10% Real Fruit Juice."

Empower Yourself!

1. Remember that food companies place images on labels to attract you to their products while you are shopping. Always read the product name to make sure you know what is in the package and refer to the list of ingredients for the actual contents. Remember that the ingredients are listed in descending order by weight with the heaviest (most) ingredient listed first.

2. If a label states "Enlarged to Show Texture" or similar text, keep in mind that the food you are purchasing is going to be smaller than it appears on the label. If this text is not displayed, the image should be actual size or smaller than reality.

3. Remember that graphic designers, food stylists, and professional food photographers have all worked on the images displayed on labels. For this reason, the food may not look exactly as it does in the image when it is ready to eat, and especially if it needs to be further prepared. We don't always cook our foods to a perfect golden brown colour or to the perfect temperature to have cheese melt in a wonderfully appetizing way.

Part 3

How to Effectively Read Prepackaged Processed Food Labels

CHAPTER 18

Five Steps to Reading Food Labels

LIFE HAS NEVER SEEMED TO BE MORE OF a balancing act than it does today. Everyone is so pressed for time trying to keep up with work, family, and life that we sometimes forget to stop and smell the roses, or in my world, stop and read the labels.

Like dieting, there is no "quick fix" when it comes to label reading. It is best to consider *all* elements of a food label to make an informed decision as to whether you want to put a product in your cart or leave it on the shelf. To recap, the following five steps should help you efficiently read prepackaged processed food labels while shopping. Remember that foods are labelled with information to help us make informed choices; however, food companies also use labels as marketing tools, and we have to train ourselves to look past their enticing claims and images and focus on the facts.

Step 1: Find the Product Name to Figure Out What Is in the Package

The product name on the front of the label should tell you what is in the package. Remember that not all products are created equally. Are you looking at the real deal or at an imposter product? That is, apple juice versus apple drink, or ice cream versus frozen dairy dessert.

Do not be misled by the brand name, which may include potentially misleading words such as *healthy*, *smart*, or *natural*, and remember to look past the images that are made to look as enticing as possible by food stylists, graphic designers, and professional photographers.

Step 2: Read the List of Ingredients

The most critical piece of information on the label is the list of ingredients; this tells you what is really in the product. Remember that the first ingredient is present in the greatest amount by weight, and typically, the last ingredient is present in the least amount (with exceptions).

If you notice an ingredient class name (please see chapter 7 for a list of permitted ingredient class names) or an ingredient that is exempt from declaring its component ingredients (please see chapter 8 for a list of ingredients that are exempt from declaring component ingredients), keep in mind that the food may contain additional hidden ingredients, and more specifically, additives that you may be trying to avoid. Conversely, if you see component ingredients, note that they are only a subset of the ingredient before the parentheses, and are thus listed in descending order only within the parentheses, and not within the order of the entire list of ingredients.

The Inside Scoop

Visit the "Inside Scoop" page at www.grainofsalt.ca and type in the password KNOWLEDGE to gain access. If you are concerned with the healthfulness of an ingredient, refer to the "Ingredients" section for a list of helpful food additive dictionaries and applications.

 ## Did you know?

If you are concerned about synthetic ingredients, synthetic preservatives, synthetic pesticides, genetically modified foods, synthetic growth regulators (including hormones), and irradiation, simply buy organic! Organic foods sold in Canada are not permitted to contain any of these ingredients, or ingredients that have been treated using these methods (with some exceptions);* therefore, reading the list of ingredients often becomes a much less daunting task. Keep in mind, however, that the term *organic* does not refer to a specific level of healthfulness of a product regarding its nutrient content. Prepackaged processed organic foods can still have high levels of fat, sodium, and sugars and low levels of fibre, vitamins, and minerals.

* Canadian General Standards Board. *Organic Products Systems Permitted Substances Lists*, CAN/CGSB-32.311-2006, amended August 2011, and *Organic Production Systems General Principles and Management Standards* 1.4, "Prohibited Substances, Methods or Ingredients in Organic Production and Handling." CAN/CGSB-32.310-2006, amended October 2008.

Step 3: Read the Nutrition Facts Table

Some may argue that the nutrition facts table is more important than the list of ingredients, and in some instances they may be right; either way, the nutrient amounts listed in the nutrition facts table can have a huge influence on your health and should be considered each time you read a label.

Remember to always look at the serving size first to gain a clear understanding of how much of the food the nutrient amounts and per cent daily values are referring to. You may want to flip the package over and review the net quantity statement on the front of the package if you are planning to eat half or the whole package at once. If you do eat more than the suggested serving size indicated, you will need to multiply the nutrition facts table amounts and per cent daily values accordingly.

Per cent daily values are a great way to calculate how much of a certain nutrient you have consumed on a specific day as compared with recommended daily intakes and reference standards, but remember they are based on an average Canadian adult consuming 2,000 calories a day. If your calorie needs are lower or higher, the per cent daily values will have to be adjusted accordingly. Also remember that the reference standard for sodium (2,400 mg) is not reflective of Health Canada's recommended intake for sodium of 1,000 mg to 1,500 mg per day for people over the age of one.[1]

---

1 Health Canada. "Sodium: Questions and Answers: What Is the Recommended Intake?" December 29, 2010, www.hc-sc.gc.ca/fn-an/nutrition/sodium/qa-sodium-qr-eng.php#a4.

Did you know?

If you tend to focus only on the calorie and fat amounts, try considering some additional nutrients. It is common for sodium and sugars amounts to be high in foods that have been modified to remove or lower the food's fat content. Talk to your health-care provider about how much of each nutrient you should be consuming daily based on your individual needs, and try to stay within those limits.

Step 4: Read Any Additional Information with a Grain of Salt

Look for any claims that may be on the label. Claims are permitted to be displayed anywhere on the label except for the bottom of the package. Compare these claims to determine if one product appeals to you more than the other; for example, does one product claim to contain 100 per cent whole wheat, while the other claims only to be made with whole wheat? Does one product claim to be low in fat, while the other claims to be fat-free? Does one product claim to be free of artificial flavours and colours, while the other claims only to be free of artificial flavours?

Go back and take a second look at the list of ingredients and the nutrition facts table. Judge for yourself whether or not these claims appear to be accurate and truthful.

Step 5: Don't Fall Victim to
Misleading Information on Food Labels

If you have questions concerning any information displayed on your food labels, find the dealer name and address information and use it. Contact the manufacturer, importer, or distributor to clarify any questions or concerns you may have.

During university, I worked as a summer student in the customer service department for a large Canadian food company. It was my job to clarify information on the labels as well as to log consumer complaints. You may think one consumer cannot make a difference, but let me reassure you that I saw claims pulled off labels and artwork changed based on consumer concerns.

If a food company cannot answer your questions concerning ingredients because they consider the information to be proprietary, chances are it may also be because they know you will not like what you hear.

Remember that you can also contact the CFIA if you believe a label displays information that you feel is misleading or potentially fraudulent. In doing so, you will not only be protecting yourself, but you will also be protecting other Canadians who may not be as informed.

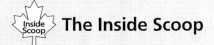 **The Inside Scoop**

Visit the the "Inside Scoop" page at www.grainofsalt.ca and type in the password KNOWLEDGE to gain access. Refer to the "Speak Up!" section for instructions on how to contact the CFIA.

Ultimately, you are in charge of which foods you decide to buy and eat. If you do not feel comfortable with the information that is displayed on a prepackaged processed food label, I strongly encourage you to leave the product on the shelf and move on to a product that you do feel comfortable with. As an insider, I hope you will join me on my mission to decode food labels for Canadian consumers by sharing the information in this book with those who may be confused, frustrated, and overwhelmed. Together we can make a difference!

Index